For GOD and COUNTRY [in that order]

FAITH AND SERVICE FOR ORDINARY RADICALS

Logan Mehl-Laituri

Herald Press
Waterloo, Ontario
Harrisonburg, Virginia

Library of Congress Cataloging-in-Publication Data
Mehl-Laituri, Logan, 1981-
For God & country (in that order) : faith & service for ordinary radicals / by Logan Mehl-Laituri.
pages cm
Includes bibliographical references.
ISBN 978-0-8361-9630-6 (pbk.)
1. Soldiers--Religious life. I. Title. II. Title: For God and country (in that order).
BV4588.M435 2013
270.092'2--dc23
2013025016

FOR GOD AND COUNTRY (IN THAT ORDER)

Library of Congress Control Number: 2013025016
International Standard Book Number: 978-0-8361-9630-6
Printed in United States of America
Cover design by Merrill Miller
Interior design and layout by Reuben Graham

To order or request information, please call 1-800-245-7894 in the U.S. or 1-800-631-6535 in Canada. Or visit www.HeraldPress.com.

17 16 15 14 13 10 9 8 7 6 5 4 3 2 1

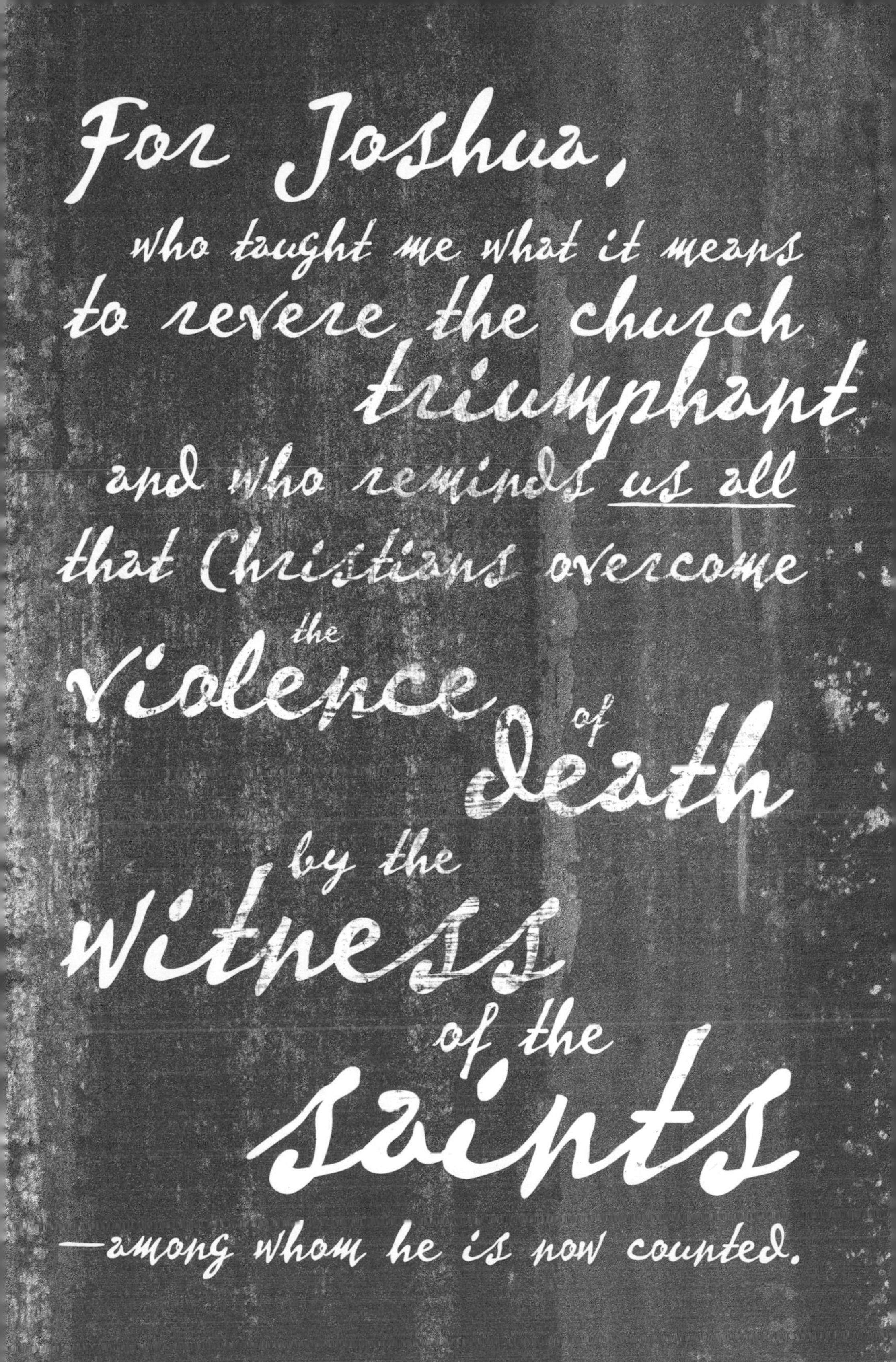
For Joshua,
who taught me what it means
to revere the church
triumphant
and who reminds us all
that Christians overcome
the
violence
of
death
by the
witness
of the
saints
—among whom he is now counted.

Contents

Part III: Pacifists and Pacific Patriots

Appendixes

Foreword

By Jonathan Wilson-Hartgrove

When the apostle Paul, an inmate in the Roman prison system, looked to his captor's armor for a metaphor of how faith can guard and keep a soul in this life, he was engaging in a deeply subversive act. Following the way of his Lord, Paul turned the world upside down to practice kingdom values, beating swords into plowshares by redeeming the very symbols of oppression for the ultimate freedom movement.

Somehow, two thousand years later, young people in vacation Bible schools throughout the Bible Belt pledge allegiance to the flag before they pledge allegiance to the Bible, singing "I'm in the Lord's Army" before they bow to pray for the success of Americans in the ongoing war on terror.

On a recent trip to Nashville, Tennessee, I heard a story about a July Fourth weekend service at a megachurch where Army Green Berets rappelled from the ceiling of the auditorium as patriotic songs played through the loudspeakers. On the screen, I was told, a verse of Scripture appeared: "Greater love hath no man than this, that a man lay down his life for his friends."

Somehow Christendom has taken the subversive military metaphors of Scripture and used them to justify the very thing Christ came to save us from. Somehow, we've turned the great sacrifice of our Lord into a slogan for our troops.

But however pervasive this tragic distortion of our tradition may be, it is not total. There are now, as there have been throughout the ages, people who have read the Bible and heard its gospel, turning from the false hope of this world and its powers to the good news that another way is possible.

Despite the mixed story of Christian history, God has sent us exemplary Christians in every generation. Traditionally, the church calls these witnesses saints. Very often, they are people whom God has called to put down their sword and take up their cross.

The stories Logan has recorded in this book are so important because they remind us what the heart of the gospel is—the hope that a better way is possible in this world. What's more, these stories are essential because they remind us that no one is beyond redemption. Just as Paul transformed the Roman armor into a metaphor for faith, God has called soldiers from the armies of this world to join the struggle for peace and justice that can only be fought with weapons of the spirit.

These stories help us to see how sometimes soldiers make the best saints. I'm reminded of what Gandhi said about soldiers, reflecting on his own service as a medic during the Boer War of South Africa. "There is some hope that a soldier will become a *satyagrahi* [a practitioner of nonviolence]," Gandhi said. "But there is no hope that a coward will."

God, give us grace to learn from these stories the courage that is required of true soldiers in the Lord's army.

—Jonathan Wilson-Hartgrove
Speaker and author of *The New Monasticism*

Preamble

"We the people" opens one of the world's most audacious documents. The Constitution of the United States of America is a living document, which citizens constantly look to for guidance, to interpret, and when necessary, to revise. American soldiers swear to protect this document against all enemies, foreign and domestic. As a living text, it is not perfect. When it was written "we" were Christian, white, land-owning men; women, enslaved people, and those without real estate were implicitly excluded. Since then, the "we" has been expanded to include others.

Today, the "we" is not necessarily Christian, and to be a citizen does not require religious affiliation. This might seem obvious, but some in the church are learning the hard way that the line between God and country is not a clear set of footprints in the sand, but a path that diverges in the woods. These Christians find themselves in military service to their country and yet struggling to reconcile their love for God and their love for their country. Some lean toward pacifism, and some believe in "just war." The military members of "we the people" are often left beaten along the road to Jericho, wounded and in need of assistance.[1] Ironically, they also belong to the same line of people who brought walls tumbling down under Joshua's command.[2]

This book follows close on the heels of my first book, *Reborn on the Fourth of July: The Challenge of Faith, Patriotism, and Conscience.*[3]

1. The parable of the good Samaritan is found in Luke 10:29-37. The man left beaten is a traveler on the road to Jericho.
2. The story of the fall of Jericho to the Israelites is in the book of Joshua, chapters 2 to 6. At the end of my *Reborn on the Fourth of July*, I compared the wounded traveler of Luke to Christian soldiers trying to find their way back from the hell of war. Military experience creates a unique perspective and lens that often shapes an entire life, for good or for ill. This book serves as a kind of narrative reader for the church to think through what the fruit of such lives can look like.
3. InterVarsity, 2012.

Writing *Reborn*, a story of my conversion while serving as a soldier, was not possible without immersing myself in the work of God in the lives of other soldiers. The lives of Christian saints and soldiers encouraged, challenged, and intrigued me. Their lives made clear to me that these were people I am called to serve—and to whom the entire church is called as well.

This awareness was also a heavy burden. I saw many Christians and churches insulated and cut off from the deep moral and spiritual pain that our service members endure. As General Sherman famously said following the siege of Atlanta during the American Civil War, "War is hell." Indeed, many of the "we the people" who make up the martial fraternity revisit hell often, usually against our will. Some of us are dragged back kicking and screaming in the middle of our nightmarish posttrauma symptoms, sleeping or waking. Those comrades, soldiers past and present, have been falling upon their own swords at far greater rates than have fallen "by the sword"[4] in battle. They linger near the gates of hell, on that fiery road to Jericho they know so well. That some veterans have seen the hell of war and yet believe in God is nothing short of a miracle.

Though not true of many soldiers today, my travels to hell were voluntary. One of the good and just virtues my military training taught me was never to leave a fallen comrade behind. In my years of researching and writing for my first book and now this one, I heard God calling me to where I did not want to go, like Jonah to Nineveh. The terrible wisdom made possible by my time so close to the gates of hell felt far more a curse than a blessing, but God has worked in mysterious ways through it all.

I am a member of an unconventional body within the historical church that defies easy categorization as good or evil: soldiers who seek to honor God. We hunted Jesus shortly after his birth[5] and watched

4. Matthew 26:52.
5. Matthew 2:16.

when he was baptized in the river Jordan.[6] One of our number showed greater faith than all of Israel,[7] while another pierced Jesus' side at Golgotha.[8] Still, countless vets and soldiers whisper to one another of their hidden loneliness, of how churches have been overwriting their lamentable experiences with glory and veneration. Or else, not having encouraged military service in the first place, the churches have offered only penetrating and unforgiving silence.

We, this people, Christian men and women of the martial experience, are legion. Being many means that we are never alone. But this is not a book for soldiers; it is a book for the church. Our healing is bound up in that of God's people across the centuries and across national borders. Church history starts looking like Swiss cheese if you take away the presence of her soldier saints and patriot pacifists. In his *Confessions* Saint Augustine of Hippo coined the term *ex pluribus unum*—"from the many, one"—and the phrase aptly describes today's Christian community. Our stories as soldiers are integral to our story as Christians.

As the early church grew, so did her soldiers and their unconventional faith. We were the first communal monks,[9] one of us founded the single largest order of priests and lay brothers,[10] and another of us is among the most venerated religious figures in history.[11] We've gone to war weaponless and been featured in major motion pictures.[12] We are not always in the places and times you might expect.

On one recent Veterans Day, which fell on a Sunday, a local pastor changed her sermon at the last minute to accommodate my frantic pleas that former soldiers be acknowledged somehow in the midst of

---

6. Luke 3:14.
7. See pp. 41–43, on the centurion of great faith in Matthew's and Luke's gospels.
8. See pp. 44–47, on the soldier known as Saint Longinus.
9. See pp. 84–86, on Saint Pachomius, the first communal monk.
10. See pp. 101–104, on Saint Ignatius of Loyola, who founded the Jesuits.
11. See pp. 91–93, on Saint Francis of Assisi, who founded the Franciscans.
12. Chaplain Francis Sampson, for example, who provided the basis for Steven Spielberg's *Saving Private Ryan*.

worship. I could tell the part she altered when she paused momentarily to meet eyes with me and wink, as though she was doing me a favor. But the favor was not for me, or even for veterans; it was for the church. Without acknowledging our soldiers, ancient and contemporary, we do our traditions and our Scripture a grave disservice.

A church wearied by doctrinal disputes and political mudslinging is still befuddled by this cry from the wilderness that Cain wandered before us: "Our burden is too great!"[13] The church is never too big or too busy to tend to the least among us, the 1 percent of Americans who have served during the "global war on terror." The same soldiers who swear, by God, to protect our cherished institutions, like the Constitution, the Crown, or the Commonwealth, sometimes find that in following their country, they're being led away from God—led, not by the devil, but by Christians who have bigger or better causes to promote, larger checks to write, and greater distances to travel to find those in need. But in the words of one soldier, "These [soldiers] are the people who desperately need Christ, and you don't have to search third-world countries to find them; they are the neighbors we have in this nation."

The church owes her soldiers no favors. But the church owes itself the truth that soldiers and their stories are part of our heritage of faith. The ancient centurion and the contemporary soldier bleed together; they are of one spirit. Their martial fraternity spans human history. It is through duty-bound soldiers that the church may most fully recognize those who killed our Lord, Jesus Christ. The same person who would shout, "Crucify, crucify, crucify" with the mob will yell, "Kill, kill, kill" on the bayonet range. That person is you. It is I. It is the "we the people" who, paradoxically, constitute the body of Christ.

---

13. Genesis 4:13, author's paraphrase. For more parallels between Cain and his contemporary counterparts, see my testimony for "Jesus, Bombs, and Ice Cream" on Sep. 11, 2011; http://loganmehllaituri.com/video/jesus-bombs-ice-cream-testimony/.

Style, Biases, *and* Other Disclaimers

An academic advisor of mine once told me, "Don't write academically." I wasn't sure what to make of this, since I was in the midst of an academic degree at an academically rigorous seminary. But I have tried to take his rather unexpected advice to heart. My service is not ultimately to the academy itself, but to the church, so if I am unable to translate academic jargon into something the children in Sunday school will understand, I wonder about the value of such "knowledge."

Another piece of advice came from a wise woman who often admonished me to "confess [my] biases." Being both a veteran and a pacifist has inarguably shaped my reading and telling of these stories. You might notice that my biases are reflected in this book: most profiles are of people who are white, heterosexual males of European or American descent, able-bodied, and "high church" leaning, like me. This might seem to imply that the stories of gay people or people of color, women, the disabled, Orthodox, or nondenominational are less important. This cannot be further from the truth. In fact, if I could change one thing about this book, it would be to have had more energy and time to develop the included stories more fully and to find more diverse voices to feature. Alas, that must wait for a second volume.

The genre of this book is partly an almanac. It is a series of self-contained historical accounts and anecdotes that help to inform practitioners of a particular field. Farmers use almanacs to help determine planting dates, surfers consult them for tide ranges, astronomers record within them phases of the moon and stars, and Biff Tannen used one to get rich gambling in sports.[1] Their purpose, however, is not simply to record, but to help us see better where the future is heading, at least in the short term. Much of the material in almanacs has to do with seasons, celestial bodies, and tidal changes, based on past patterns. Likewise, in the church, to see our path more clearly we must turn to our own history. And I find that that history includes voices and perspectives that may not reflect my pacifist inclinations, yet shed light on what it means to be a people of peace. I hope this book may be a resource not just to pacifists, but also to those within the military or otherwise associated with it, trying to discern what it means to love God and country.

For God and Country is not only an almanac; it is something like hagiography—a collection of stories about the lives of holy people. Other hagiographies that you might know of would be *Foxe's Book of Martyrs* of 1563, Thieleman van Braght's *Martyrs Mirror* of 1660, or *Butler's Lives of the Saints* from the 1750s.[2] Each of these was produced by and reflects a beautiful diversity. John Foxe was a Protestant preacher, Thieleman was an Anabaptist, and Butler was a Catholic priest. In each case, their distinct convictions and perspectives shaped their selection of profiles, though each account provides an indispensable resource for the entire church.

This book does the same. The profiles are short and self-contained; you can pick up the book for an afternoon, or just during commercial breaks. Don't feel compelled to read this book cover to cover. I will not be insulted if I spy your copy sitting atop your toilet. While I did

---

1. *Back to the Future Part II* (Universal, 1989).
2. See the bibliography on page 217 to learn how to access these resources in print or online.

not intend to write a devotional, I do include some prayers and some personal reflections; I would be surprised if nobody ever used this book as a kind of devotional.

This book reflects my persistent sense that I sometimes feel more at home with other veterans and service members of faith than I do with the folks I sit next to on Sundays. If we are a subgroup within the global church, this book might be a start at our own hagiography—one that features the lives of those pathfinders whose lives were shaped by their military experience.

Because it is so shaped, those with military experience will read this book somewhat differently than their civilian counterparts, especially in my sporadic use of military terms. Where appropriate, I try to offer footnotes and explanations of those terms. Even so, if you are not a military person, I encourage you to find someone you trust who has served in the military and read this book with them. If you do not know anyone with military experience, consider that an area of your life that could use some enriching. Just as the army always taught us never to do anything without a battle buddy, the church lives and reads in community.

My only regret in compiling this hagiographic almanac is discovering its limits; much more can and should be said about each profile, and many more similar profiles could and should be written. Consider the profiles here as introductory; in many cases volumes have been written about them. On the other hand, many times I encountered conflicting reports and had to decide to privilege one account over another. While this book has some academic traction, it is really a primer intended for the broader church.

Finally, a word about death in these pages. During the writing of this work, as with my last, a friend died and I was forced to think critically about the failure of death to have the last word. When a Christian dies, it is not the end, but the beginning, one of many steps toward

resurrection. Those of us who remain here and are vigilant in our faith and service are what some traditions call "the church militant"; we still struggle against sin, the devil, and "the rulers of the darkness of this world, against spiritual wickedness in high places."[3] When our physical bodies expire, we leave the ranks of the living and enter "the church triumphant." If we truly believe that death has been conquered, then we have cause for hope. For this reason, those profiled here are arranged in the order they died, not the day they were born. For those formally recognized as saints, the days of their deaths are known as "feast days"—days to come together and remember what that holy person taught us, how they affected and continue to affect our lives. In this way, we continue to conquer death's sting, swallowing it up in God's victory.[4]

3. Ephesians 6:12 KJV.
4. Isaiah 25:6-8 KJV.

Part I
Warriors *of the* Bible

Any exploration of the soldiers who make up the church must start with those found in the Bible itself. The following profiles are the product of a weeks-long Bible study with fellow seminarians and friends. Like the stories of parts 2 and 3, they reflect our pacifist inclinations, but also the perspectives of our active duty and veteran friends. The folks featured in this segment are only a few of the many in the Bible who are soldiers of some sort, though not usually in the same sense that contemporary military personnel are.

None of the Israelites fleeing Egypt had military training; they were former slaves armed only with tools they used building storehouses for Pharaoh. Being organized into "companies" of men was less a defense mechanism than it was a means of organization for distributing common goods like land and food. Because the kingdoms and armies that eventually arose did so over large periods of time, who can say precisely what made up the military of ancient Israel, or which characters were soldiers and which were civilians?

"Because the kingdoms and armies that eventually arose did so over large periods of time, who can say precisely which characters were soldiers and which were civilians?"

While I was doing the Bible study for these profiles, I was also taking tango lessons. Dancing is not my thing; I stepped on my partner's toes, we got in fights about who was worse at the moves we were taught, and it just generally tried my patience. I had it in my head that there was a right and wrong way to tango. That is true and false. Our instructor would cringe when we did get it wrong, but tango is also not a static, unchanging formula—it is dynamic and responsive; there is no absolutely right way to do it. Interpreting our Scriptures is like that.

It is sometimes helpful to take a proverbial step back to look at the story and the times in which it was written. By not citing specific verses, I hope that these retellings will inspire you to read with Bible in hand. Dig into that good Book of ours when you see something that fires you up. For the next several pages, when I step in a certain direction, don't be afraid to push back. Scribble in the margins of this book *and* of that Bible in your hand. We're in this together as we feel out this thing we call faith. Dance with me. ☧

"Tango is not a static, unchanging formula—it is dynamic and responsive. Interpreting our Scriptures is like that."

Joshua

Book of Joshua

Joshua was a great leader and the people of Israel looked up to him. Many think that this was because he was "strong and courageous."[1] What made him great, however, was not that he valiantly commanded, but that he humbly obeyed. Joshua looked up to someone higher than himself. His humble obedience gave him qualities worthy of leading the people of God, since for them to take the land God promised, they needed to trust and obey not Joshua personally, but God. Joshua did his best to remember that God was greater, especially in responding to the call to obey God in doing violence.

"Commands worthy of being obeyed are derived from the authority of the person who makes the command."

The story of Jericho is always troubling to read. Violence in the Old Testament is as difficult to understand as it is anywhere else.[2] The Bible

---

1. Joshua 1:6, 7, and 9. In verse 9, it is clear God is in charge; "Have *I* not commanded *you*?"
2. For particularly helpful reflections, see Patricia MacDonald, *God and Violence: Biblical Resources for Living in a Small World* (Scottdale, PA: Herald Press, 2004). She has a very insightful chapter on the book of Joshua that should not be overlooked.

shows us that violence tends to get out of hand quickly. Soldiers need oversight and guidance from strong and courageous leaders unwilling to give in to passionate excess, leaders who know that obedience itself is not a virtue. Commands worthy of being obeyed are derived from the authority of the person who makes the command. At Jericho, it was not ultimately Joshua commanding the hosts of Israel, but God.

Furthermore, to call what Joshua oversaw "violence" threatens to confuse our context for his. For example, in our own day, it doesn't seem like sound military strategy to ask the Marine Corps Band to lead a battalion or two around Baghdad (or Saigon or Berlin for that matter) to attain victory. At best, Jericho is an example of a liturgical parade, and the destruction that followed was carefully limited. In fact, when it was found out later that a man named Achan had violated the rules of engagement by taking war trophies, he was killed in order to restore the integrity of the religious community. Joshua was merely God's instrument; Achan disobeyed God, the commander in chief.

Comparing Joshua to a modern military commander is at best a half truth. Joshua would need to be thought of as an orchestra conductor and clerical priest, to name one or two additional roles. In fact, before the Jericho pageant begins, Joshua is visited by an angelic being who calls himself "the commander of the Lord's army."[3] That the angel assumes the title means that the title does not belong to Joshua. In fact the angel scolds Joshua for assuming that he is on one side or another, since siding with God means not taking sides in the first place. When Joshua assumes that this angel of God is either for him or against him, he is rebuked. "Neither!" replies the unnamed

3. See the end of Joshua 5 for this exchange.

angel. Indeed, the true fight is not between men on the battlefield, but within people's hearts. For as the book of James says, "What causes fights and quarrels among you? Don't they come from your desires that battle within *you*?"[4]

★ ★ ★

Our disordered loves and our tendency toward sin are what cause havoc in our world. Every human enemy of ours is, as much as we are, a participant in, and a victim of, the real but invisible war raging in us all. This is what the angel is saying: God's heavenly hosts do not pit humans against humans in cosmic battle. They are on God's side only. Christian obedience is measured by its conformity to the command and nature of God, not necessarily the human officers appointed above us.

"Siding with God means not taking sides in the first place."

God doesn't need hate speeches or propaganda, attack ads or sloganeering. These things serve only the desires at war within us: to be right, to be in charge, to be God. We must remember Jericho as not only that place in the Old Testament where the people of God brought the walls tumbling down, but also that place in the New Testament where the good Samaritan encounters the wounded stranger in need of healing.[5] We are not God; we are the ones in need of healing from what we must do in trying to restore order and peace in our violent world. It takes courage and strength to be humble and attentive to the God who is not only our own, but our enemy's. Joshua was indeed a strong and courageous leader, but it was his obedience to the command of God that defined his command.

4. James 4:1, emphasis added.
5. Luke 10:29-37.

DEBORAH

Judges 4–5

Sometimes we get in our heads that soldiering and statecraft is a man's game that just takes a certain kind of tenacity and stoicism to pull off effectively. Don't tell that to Deborah or Jael.

Once the Promised Land was relatively settled, it fell to the Israelites to govern themselves. Before kings were appointed, the twelve tribes of Israel were a loose confederation of clans, not organized by any modern means. Judges were those people who emerged in times of crisis in Israel to lead the people through various ordeals like conflicts with neighbors, or settling disputes about land distribution. But judges did not just sit in court, they also might prophesy and often led in battle. They were called to duty at times of crisis, when God needed courageously obedient men and women to restore Israel from hardship.

Deborah was the fourth of about seventeen Judges mentioned in the Bible after Joshua's command.[1] She was known as "a mother of Israel" and kept court under a palm tree somewhere between Ramah and Bethel. At the time, the Canaanite king Jabin of Hazor was oppressing Israel. Deborah speaks for God by commanding Barak, another judge and the captain of the army, to lead a campaign against the Canaanites and win some measure of rest from their oppression. Barak insists that Deborah go with him in the campaign, so Deborah gears up and

1. Including Joshua, Othniel, Ehud, Shamgar, Barak, Gideon, Abimilech, Tola, Jair, Jephthah, Ibzan, Elon, Abdon, Samson, Fli, and Samuol.

heads out to battle. However, she prophesies that because she is with Barak, the honor of the victory will go not to him, but to a woman.

When the enemy commander Sisera retreats toward his family's camp, he comes upon the tent of the Kenite woman Jael. The Kenites had descended from Moses's brother-in-law, Hobab, but had made an alliance with Jabin, Sisera's king. Israel was her family, the family of God, but she was aligned politically with Jabin, her family's oppressors. Sisera demands he be given sustenance and that Jael keep watch while he sleeps and recovers his strength. Left to choose between familial and political allegiances, Jael feigns compliance with a sip of milk, only to kill him in his sleep and secure the victory for Israel in the meantime. Deborah's prophecy is fulfilled; the honor of the victory goes to a woman—Jael.

★ ★ ★

Women in modern armies frequently have been forbidden from serving in frontline capacities, such as the infantry or artillery. Because of the prestige that these branches receive, the prohibition implies a lower status of women. In Christianity more broadly, women have been marginalized and neglected in biblical interpretation and theological studies alike. But this is neither biblical nor theologically sound, since women have held positions equal to those held by men, including those of judge (Deborah), scholar (Priscilla, Acts 18), and apostle (Junia, Romans 16). Miriam courageously disobeyed her head of state, with Shiphrah and Puah, to save her little brother Moses and many other Hebrew babies. Some women even stand head and shoulders above men, like Esther, who has her own book in the Bible (like Joshua) and saved the Jews of Persia; and Mary, who bore Jesus and whom Roman Catholics call "Mother of God."

"Those who lead God's people, like Joshua and Deborah, are not worthy commanders because of what they have between their hips, but because of what they display within their hearts."

Sometimes the church imitates the world, however, and at times unconsciously fails to speak prophetically against treating women as subordinate objects. For example, why have so few sermons been preached on the unnamed concubine of Judges 19?[2] The Levite who cast her into the street to be raped was the religious figure of the day, a leader of the people of God. Those who lead God's people, like Joshua and Deborah, are not worthy commanders because of what they have between their hips, but because of what they display within their hearts. If we say that apostles are our models for ordination, Junia is troublingly absent in many debates on the ordination of women.

Women have been as bold and memorable as men—we just don't always realize it. After all, women have graced the pages of the Bible as much as they have the pages of history; it's time scholars took a closer look to see what more women have to teach the fields of military and theological studies.

2. It would be ironic to recount the story here, as my point is that far too few men, who make up a majority of priests, pastors, theologians, and scholars, and who self-identify as the heads of households, know stories like this enough to be enraged about them. The concubine is especially relevant to those interested in war, as Judges 20 recounts a war fought in her (unmentioned) name. Read it, talk about it, and be righteously upset that women in the Bible and in your community are treated this way.

During my very first jump in the 82nd Airborne Division, I remember how much my heart raced. I was afraid; would my static line tangle around me as I exited the door? Would I hit another paratrooper in the air? Would I be injured during my parachute landing fall? Before we got the command "Stand up, hook up!" a wise old paratrooper saw the fear in my eyes and told me, "It's okay to be scared, private. We all are. It's when you aren't nervous anymore that you should worry." Fear is always with us, especially on the battlefield. Courage is not the absence of fear; it describes those who act despite fear, who let *nothing* stand in the way of doing what is right.

> *"Courage is not the absence of fear; it describes those who act despite fear."*

In a time when all of Israel did things offensive to God, when everyone did what was good only for themselves, an angel of God visits a young man and greets him with the words "The Lord is with you, mighty warrior." But Gideon protests, saying humbly "My clan is the weakest . . . and I am the least in my family." Little does he know that God uses the lowly, that the best soldiers rarely think too highly of themselves.

Once God has given Gideon reason to believe otherwise, the warrior-to-be makes an altar to God and names the place "The Lord Is Peace." He is not your typical soldier, at least not at first. For starters, he is

rather sheepish; when he sees the angel of the Lord, he is afraid he will die. When told to destroy an idol for God, he is afraid of the wrath of the town in which it sits. Finally, he is afraid of the enemies he will encounter in battle.

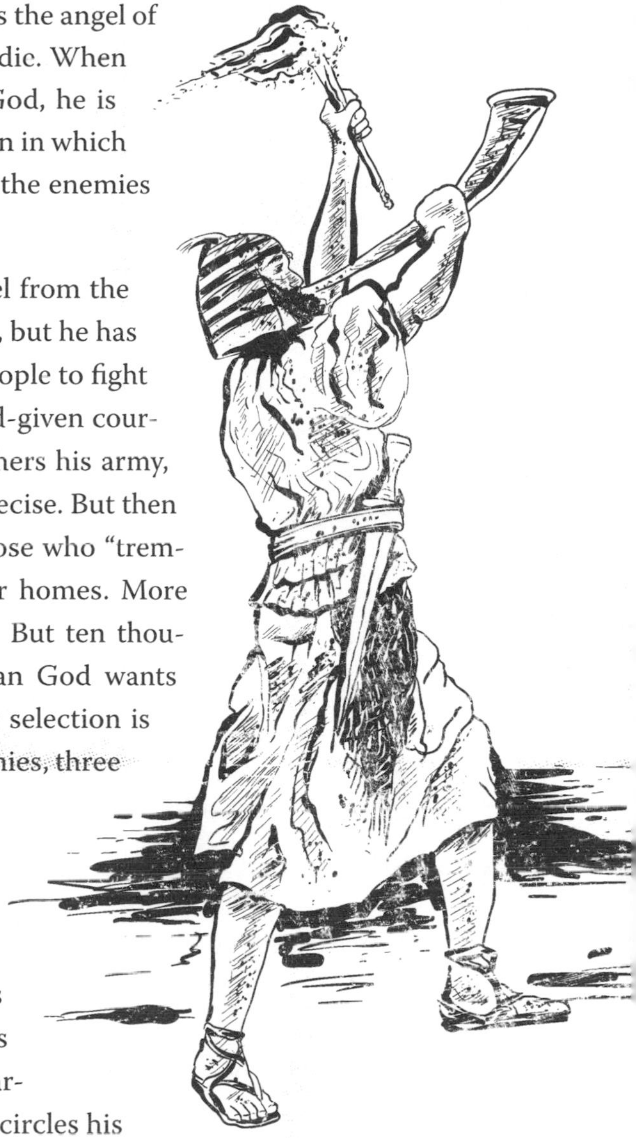

Gideon is called to free Israel from the oppression of the Midianites, but he has yet to learn that God asks people to fight in peculiar ways. With a God-given courage in his heart, Gideon gathers his army, thirty-two thousand to be precise. But then God tells Gideon to send those who "trembled with fear" back to their homes. More than half pick up and leave. But ten thousand men are still more than God wants on Gideon's side, so another selection is made; this time three companies, three hundred men, are left.

On the eve of battle, Gideon is still nervous, but he hears the enemy speak about being afraid, thanks to a dream one of them has had. In a scene echoing an earlier battle by Joshua, Gideon circles his enemy's camp and the three hundred men blow trumpets and break clay jars containing their torches. In the meantime, God confuses their enemies, leaving the Midianites to destroy one another in the confusion. Gideon's companies, not even a battalion, have won the fight God asked of them. But then they go beyond the orders they are given and pursue the Midianites without mercy. God is no longer before them, but behind them—silent, right there at the camp they are told to take and keep. A healthy fear of the Lord leaves Gideon, and he replaces it with a hearty dose of vengeance and vainglory.

"The best soldiers rarely think too highly of themselves."

As the dust settles and Gideon's bloodthirst leaves the kings of Midian at his feet, he insists his young son finish off the royal party with his sword. But the boy is afraid, just as Gideon once was. His innocent fear brings Gideon back to his senses; his rampage is capped with an attempt to return to God's good graces. Gideon uses gold volunteered by the warriors to build a memorial of God's deliverance from the Midianites. The fear of the Lord returns, and the land experiences rest for forty years.

★ ★ ★

It's okay to be afraid, no matter the situation. Returning home is never a walk of shame, as twenty-two thousand men learned before that battle with Midian. But sometimes you step, trembling, onto the field of battle despite your fear. You'll still have your anxieties, but you trust in God's strength for your own, and you never do more than you're asked, never overstep the restraint inherent in lawful orders. Fear must never give way to anger or retribution, lest God use the weak to shame the vengeful; the young and untested to shame the blind arrogance of the battle-hardened.

"You'll still have your anxieties, but you trust in God's strength for your own, and you never overstep the restraint inherent in lawful orders."

Samson

Judges 13–16

Samson, the third to last judge of Israel before the nation was ruled by kings, is invariably referred to as a hero or a mighty warrior. But a close look at his story makes one wonder whether it's about his strengths or his weaknesses. God visits his mother as an angel and instructs her that her son will be a Nazirite, a special Jewish vocation. Nazirites make vows to abstain from alcohol, avoid corpses, and keep from cutting their hair. His unnamed mother agrees to the terms and Samson is given the great strength for which he is known, but he doesn't seem to appreciate or share his mother's piety.

He sees a Philistine woman and tells his father bluntly, "Get her for me." Before the arranged marriage, they hold a wine-feast (so much for refraining from alcohol), where he bets that he can outsmart some of his in-laws with a riddle. If they can answer the riddle within seven days, he will give them thirty sets of clothing, but if they are stumped

they must give the same number of suits to him. When they get the answer from his unnamed bride by threatening to kill her family, he slays and leaves naked thirty random men from a small town in order to make good the bet he shouldn't have made in the first place.

"His violence is the exponential and vengeful violence condemned throughout the Bible."

The first two clauses of his Nazirite oath fall like the pillars he'll later bring down in a suicidal attempt to kill the very Philistines whose community he had insisted on marrying into. His violence is not just the retributive eye-for-an-eye stuff, but the exponential and vengeful violence condemned throughout the Bible.[1] His violence is belligerent and over the top, not befitting a leader of Israel, but that of a lone wolf. In fact, the Bible doesn't mention his leadership practices in the three chapters in which he appears, except that he was a judge for twenty years.

However, Samson's supreme weakness lies not in being easily provoked or quick to anger, but his interest in women. He visits a prostitute in Gaza and then falls in love with Delilah, who does not share his feelings. Blinded by his passion long before the Philistines gouge out his eyes, soon the third clause of his Nazirite vow falls to the ground around his feet, and with it, God's covenantal obligation made to Samson's mother. After several comic opportunities to see Delilah for the conspirator she is and escape harm, Samson tells her the secret to his belligerent strength—the seven locks upon his head, left uncut as a reminder of his mother's vow to God.

Samson violates the criterion of being sober at the wine-feast wedding rehearsal dinner. He violates the second clause thirtyfold shortly thereafter, when he makes a bet based on an overestimate of his own intellectual prowess. Two times God could have deprived him of his

1. Exodus 21:23-25; Leviticus 24:19-20; and Deuteronomy 19:21, for example.

gift but didn't. Surely he must have thought, "God would not abandon me now." Incredibly, he is surprised when Delilah's betrayal deprives him of his physical prowess: "What, the Lord leave me, Samson the judge of Israel?"

Far from being an archetype of virtue, he is the antithesis of it, multiplying violence exponentially wherever he goes. When the people affected by his mischief try to bring him to justice, he defends himself by claiming he was responding in kind. Proportionality is a cornerstone of the just war tradition,[2] but one bet is not proportionate to thirty men. When men came to bring him to justice, Samson kills one thousand with a donkey's jawbone, which he uses to ridicule the very people who came trying to enforce the peace. His last act is a suicide-murder that kills three thousand enemies—in effect gouging out six thousand more eyes for the two eyes he lost to their violence earlier. "Eye for an eye" has left thousands blind, as Samson seems to think his arrogance justifies any violence he commits. The inclusion of Samson in Scripture as Judge who ruled Israel at a time when "everyone did what was right in their own eyes" does not imply a commendation; here it is the sharpest of critiques. In fact, the chapter that introduces Samson begins with the line "Again the Israelites did evil in the eyes of the Lord."[3]

★ ★ ★

2. See page 206 for a discussion of the "just war."
3. Judges 13:1.

Not everyone who serves does so honorably, even if at first glance we might think so. I grew up hearing about "mighty Samson," but when I read the story myself, it really disturbed me. The same can be said of our military heroes; sometimes their stories can get polished in the retelling. However, honesty requires us to be forthcoming about the failures of our leaders, regardless of how highly we think of them based on their rank or anything else. That is not to say that soldiers and generals are inherently good or bad, since that is exactly the point I want to object to. We are all subject to our ego, our ambition, and our weaknesses; acknowledging that makes us more human, not less.

"The inclusion of Samson in Scripture as judge who ruled Israel at a time when 'everyone did what was right in their own eyes' does not imply a commendation; here it is the sharpest of critiques."

" I believe Christianity in America doesn't do god any justice."

thought about "what God has written"

"while watching a video during a marin

Major's brief about the USMC. The video showed helicopters dropping bombs on Iraq. . . I couldn't help but think about the lives that were there, about **children playing in the street** and families going about their day when those bombs were dropped

. . . I told (my roommate) that I felt bad

for all the lives that were destroye

She told me that she didn't like to think about that part.

. . . I feel that these people,

many of whom have screwed up philosophies,

need God.

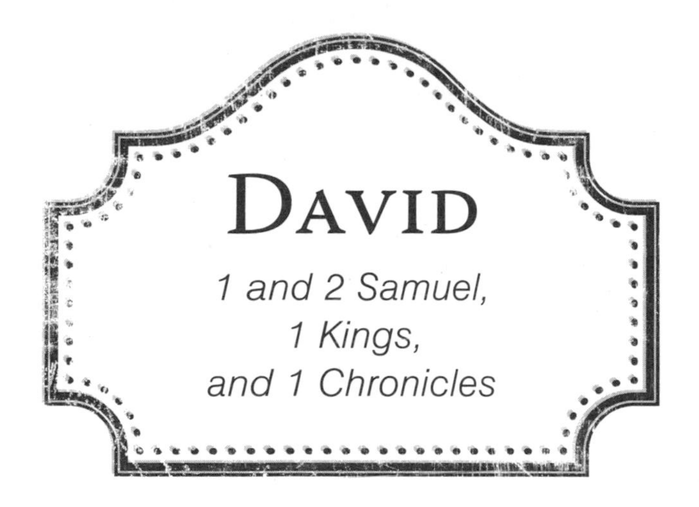

David

1 and 2 Samuel,
1 Kings,
and 1 Chronicles

Judges are not working well for Israel, and they know it. They want a king like all the other nations had, so they go to Samuel, the last judge of Israel, and insist he find them a king. Samuel prophetically warns them what a king will do; hoping the words he brings from the Lord might sway them. A king, he says, will draft their sons into war and fight behind them on the day of battle, instead of before them like God did. Kings will draft their daughters into the war effort to be seamstresses and cooks. Their land, produce, and livestock will be taken and given to members of his administration; the Israelites will become slaves. "And when you cry out to the Lord," as they did in Egypt, he tells them, "The Lord will not answer you."

The people insist, however, so God has Samuel anoint as king a man named Saul. Saul means "asked for" in Hebrew; the people got what they asked for. As king, Saul gets lofty ambitions and sees himself not as a humble servant, but the man in charge. He begins disobeying and failing to trust in God. Before a battle, he impatiently (and sacrilegiously) assumes the role of high priest and begins to make a sacrifice, and Samuel tells him that God has found another to be king, a "man after God's own heart."

As the youngest of eight boys, David was made a shepherd, which meant he relied on his herds for food all year and for warmth in the

cold months. One day when he is out in the fields Samuel visits his father, Jesse, to select a king from among Jesse's sons. David learns he will become king when, in a Cinderella moment, the judge Samuel asks to see Jesse's sons, but only seven appear. Samuel knows one is missing, and has David sent for. This unassuming shepherd boy will be the next king.

The first battlefield experience David has is against a giant who for forty days mocks his people. Goliath falls not to a deft sword or a coordinated "shock and awe" campaign, but a single rock slung from a boy's sling.[1] His courage and success in battle make the current king, Saul, jealous. Saul tries to have David killed at least twice, but when David has the chance to make sure that will never happen again by killing him first, David does not succumb to the temptation to preemptive violence. When Saul dies in battle, instead of rejoicing, David mourns his dead pursuer, becoming king.

1. As dumb as a rock may be, when wielded by the right person it appears to have been more accurate than any of our modern "smart missiles."

"David never let his failures or his successes get in the way of his relationship to God."

But David certainly has his faults. The Bible gives us a well-rounded picture of David the warrior king; he is not all roses and sunflowers, but sometimes makes grave mistakes and gives in to terrible sin. One day he sees a beautiful woman, Bathsheba. The problem is that Bathsheba was married to one of his soldiers, Uriah. Because David is king, he can send soldiers to whatever battles he chooses, even those without a high likelihood of success. He sends Uriah to one such battle so that he can have Bathsheba to himself. He doesn't even ask her thoughts on the matter; maybe she is deeply in love with Uriah, maybe she has no ambition to be with the king. The Bible makes no mention of her consent, suggesting the sin was not just adultery, but rape as well. David the warrior king wished to build the first temple to God, but God declined, saying David's hands were stained with sin and disqualified him to build the sacred house.[2]

★ ★ ★

So what does it mean that David was "a man after God's own heart?" Perhaps it means that through troubles and travails, David never let his failures or his successes get in the way of his relationship to God. When he falls short of the glory of God, he repents. When he meets great success, he attributes it to God. He burns for his maker; God is his journey as well as his destination. His heart sings for God, which is convenient since he is a talented musician. This warrior king was also a man connected to his feelings, many of which he wrote about; 73 of the 150 psalms in the Bible are supposed to be by his hand, including the psalm many warriors recite most often in contemporary battlefields, Psalm 23.

2. See 1 Chronicles 22:8-9. The task is passed to Solomon, who makes a temple one-third the size of his own palace and conveniently neglects his father's direction to employ willing skilled workers of Israel in favor of forced slave labor. See 1 Chronicles 28:21 and 1 Kings 5:13-14.

Psalm 23 has been scribbled on helmets and rifle stocks for many generations of soldiers. It was even recited by Todd Beamer during the ill-fated Flight 93 on September 11, 2001 and also during that evening's address by President George W. Bush. But it follows another psalm that Jesus recited on the cross. Psalm 22 begins "My God, my God, why have you forsaken me?" David, the most beloved king of Israel, knew that being led beside calm waters came only after moments of uncertainty. There is no joy without grief, no hope without despair. More importantly, there is no king but God. The overwhelming theme of David's psalms is God's absolute sovereignty. David believed that God, not the king or his kingdom, was "the last best hope for mankind," that the light of the world was not a state or a flag, but the people and presence of God.

NO
KING
BUT
GOD

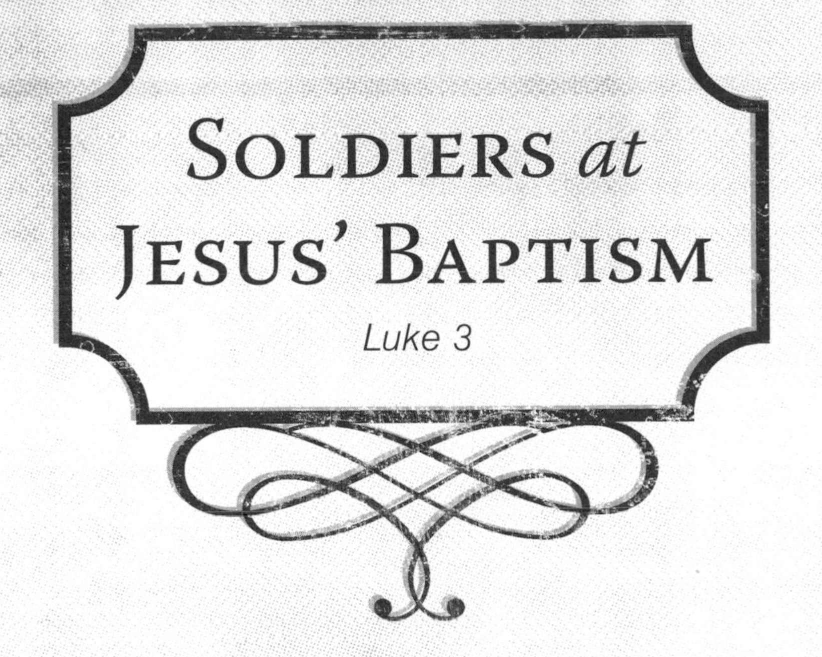

Soldiers *at* Jesus' Baptism

Luke 3

When Christians talk about soldiering, one passage that comes up often is from Jesus' baptism by John at the river Jordan. "Jesus didn't condemn the soldiers, and therefore he doesn't condemn soldiering," the line goes. What more might this tale of the unknown soldiers tell us about what is really going on?

The soldiers are likely part of a small personal security detachment accompanying the tax collector mentioned in the passage, who also received advice from John (to stop overcharging on taxes). Such associations were not uncommon. Even hated Herod Antipas had Roman soldiers assigned to protect him. The chief priests who plotted against Jesus had a temple guard who answered to the religious establishment in Jerusalem—this is why soldiers accompany them to Gethsemane to arrest Jesus (and the first place he is taken is not to Pilate, but the Sanhedrin). By no means are they conducting war, their otherwise more violent expression of statecraft. This is not a passage about war and battle, but diplomacy. They likely protected the tax collector from zealots, or enforced Rome's claim to taxes (which Jesus does not decisively challenge). The soldiers here are acting in something much

more akin to a police role; in fact, some Bible translations render the "temple guard" as "temple police."

It should not surprise us then, that God does not "bless the troops." In fact Jesus doesn't say much of anything. John, however, tells them to be content with their pay and not to falsely accuse people in order to assist the tax collector in extorting money (which tax collectors were known for). After all, as representatives of Rome, they hold all the cards; they can get away with murder, as soldiers in any age do, even today. That they even ask suggests only two possibilities: either they are taunting John, and his genuine answer undercuts their mockery with honesty, or they see this indigenous, camel-suited fool as a legitimate authority and dispenser of wisdom (which doesn't speak too highly of their armor-clad commander in chief).

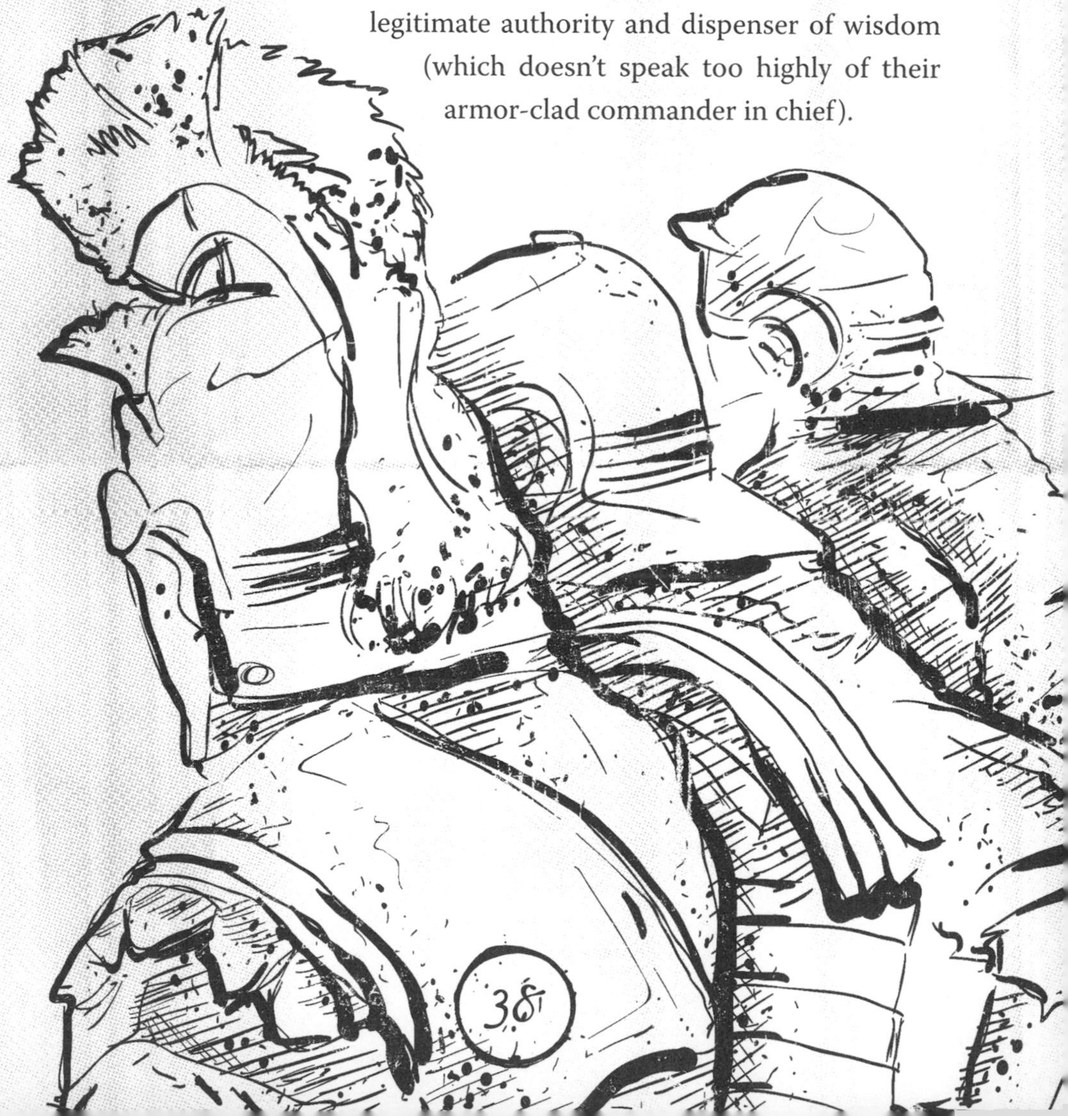

Finally, if you read the Gospels in the order they are presented in the New Testament, the answer from John the Baptizer in Luke might evoke particular stories from the earlier gospels, namely the last chapter of the book of Matthew. After Jesus is killed, the chief priests temporarily assign their temple guard to mortuary affairs, to make sure Jesus stays dead. When the tomb guards[1] report the resurrection to the chief priests, the priests tell them to falsify their report to Pilate and thereby save their skins for apparently sleeping on the job. The soldiers take the money and ominously "did as they were told," not a God-centered obedience but a self-serving one.

★ ★ ★

If Roman soldiers were generally content with their pay, would a few of them have taken the priests' money to cover up their dereliction? There might be a connection between John's warning against taking bribes and the tomb guard falsifying their report to Pilate. Corruption is rarely a character trait; most of us resort to vice only when we are in desperate need. Our families need food; our utilities have to be paid. Money is the reason that many young men and women join the army; economic factors largely sustain the modern All-Volunteer Force.[2] I've heard many stories of friends returning from war and recklessly spending all they had saved on unnecessary purchases. It's as though spending money will repair the internal issues going on inside us when we return from war. Only God can fix the hidden wounds of war, not money. We must be careful that we never pursue Mammon, the god of money, for our salvation. While we might be able to serve God and country (in that order), we "cannot serve *both* God and money."[3]

---

1. Matthew 28:11 14. "Tomb Guard" is also the name given to the prestigious unit that watches over the Tomb of the Unknown Soldier in Arlington, Virginia.
2. Even during the unpopular war in Iraq, enlistment was not substantially affected. The Army Recruiting Command officer was quoted as saying that the economy was the driver: "The chaotic conditions in Iraq have yet to hurt recruiting" (Eric Schmitt, "Soft Economy Aids Recruiting Effort," *New York Times*, Sep. 22, 2003).
3. Matthew 6:24, emphasis added.

"Only God can fix the hidden wounds of war, not money."

John's warning against bearing false witness might have something to say about the tomb guard lying to Pilate about disciples stealing Jesus' body. Soldiers would have every bit as much reason as any other person to head over to the Jordan River. At the waters of baptism, a person repents and turns away from their former lives. As fallible human beings, they have done, witnessed, and failed to prevent deeds that violate their consciences, and sometimes even the lawful orders they have been given.[4] The Baptizer has no reason to think that they are there for anything less than repentance; the time has come for a change of command[5] in their hearts.

"The Baptizer has no reason to think that they are there for anything less than repentance; the time has come for a change of command in their hearts."

4. Perpetrating, witnessing, and failing to prevent acts that violate one's moral and religious training and beliefs are major factors in predicting the onset of posttraumatic stress and moral injury. To learn more, visit http://www.britesoulrepair.org to read a 2009 report from Veterans Affairs clinicians on the emerging field of moral injury.

5. "Change of Command" is the title of the Centurions Guild community newsletter. You can read issues online at http://centurionsguild.org/resources/changeofcommand.

Centurion *of* Great Faith

Luke 7 and Matthew 8

There were many different ways to be a soldier during the Roman occupation of Palestine in the first century.[1] You could legally require a civilian to carry your gear for up to one mile. You might be assigned to a local tax collector to ensure that indigenous people paid what was due to the authorities you represented (that assignment was cushy, since your guy often cooked the books to give his team a little extra). Combat duties were relatively rare, though they did occur. The violence of the Maccabees might come to mind, or the Zealots.[2] If you were a centurion, a commander of one hundred men, you would have men under you that you ordered to go, and they went, or to come, and they came.[3] You were in charge. You called the shots.

But there is a story in Matthew and Luke about a centurion not of great pride, but of great faith. This young commander recognized in Jesus

1. The story of the centurion of great faith was very moving for me when I first began seminary. Priests quote him every week during Catholic mass just before distributing the eucharist, the bread and wine of communion, the body and blood of Jesus Christ. One week last year, I wrote a reflection on his words that I considered using for this profile, but eventually opted against it. You can read it at http://loganmehllaituri.com/2011/10/17/the-war-cry/.
2. The Maccabees were a Jewish group who violently revolted against the Seleucid Empire and succeeded in acquiring some measure of religious freedom before the Romans came in 63 BCE. *Zealot* is a generic term that includes a number of revolutionary groups in Palestine during the Roman occupation. It includes the *scicarii*, a Jewish band of "dagger men," insurrectionists who used small knives to murder political enemies in large crowds, inciting riots and terrorizing local military units.
3. Both gospels record this phrase spoken by the centurion. In Matthew, it is verse 9, and in Luke it is verse 8.

a source of much greater authority than he himself possessed, much more than Rome could grant. Matthew describes the centurion coming to Jesus to ask for healing for his servant. Jesus offers to return the favor by following him to the man's house and healing the servant. But the commander refuses, confessing that Jesus' authority is so great that only a word needed to be said, that even a man of his military stature did not deserve to have a man of such authority come under his roof: "Lord, I do not deserve to have you come under my roof. But just say the word, and my servant will be healed."

Luke takes it even further, writing that the bold and fearless warrior could not even bring himself to be in the presence of Christ. Instead, he enlists the help of Jewish elders with whom he has gained some trust. These fellow men of faith tell the great Rabbi[4] that this soldier deserves to have healing for his servant, for he loves God's people and had built a synagogue for them. So Jesus goes toward the house, only to be cut off by the centurion's friends, who relay a message to Jesus; the commander refutes the testimony of the elders, saying that he is indeed not worthy to receive Jesus. He knows what authority looks like and his pales in comparison to the Christ. But only say the word, and the man's servant shall be healed.

---

4. For all that has been said about Jesus being a person of the people, of wandering and operating at the grassroots level, it should be remembered the reason he was invited to read scripture in synagogue was that he endured the rigorous and lengthy institutional training required to be a rabbi. In a word, he was a fully ordained leader in the institutional form that religion took at that time for God's people. In another word, he was a fully credentialed authority in "the system" he challenged.

"Jesus recognized not his profession, but his humility."

This man of God did not exploit his position or boast of his power. He knew that being a soldier had its blessings as well as its curses, that the martial vocation is varied and nuanced. When he could have commanded, he bowed. Jesus recognized not his profession, but his humility.

★ ★ ★

For some, these passages might imply that the military is to be applauded, that faith and service are one in the martial fraternity. But that does not do the passage justice. The tale of this centurion is not about service as much as it is about faith. To this day, in many weekly worship services, many Christians borrow the words of the centurion just before sharing the body and blood of Christ at communion: "Lord, I am not worthy to receive you, but only say the word and I shall be healed." In this way, they embody the role of this soldier as they approach the table. This eucharistic humility makes possible our communion with Christ and with the centurion, that good and faithful servant who humbled himself as Jesus did on the cross.

Although I count myself spiritually pious,
... I am but a recovering sinner.
I constantly loathe the violence and injustice of this world
while fighting the spiritual battle in my head and heart.
... I got to work in Haiti and Costa Rica ... when I came back
I was not satisfied with my life in the US
and my new awakening to God's dream shook up the life that I already had.
... [my husband] joined the military believing the lie that
allegiance to country meant he was serving God
... He is consoled only by the words of Jesus to the centurion of great faith
and by the promise that we can be a light in this very dark place.
To live alternatively in this
militaristic system
is hard

... How do we reconcile
our lives
with our beliefs?

Longinus*[1]

Matthew 27, Mark 15, John 19

The book of John gives no name to the soldiers who arrest, abuse, and crucify Jesus. Maybe it is better that way; maybe it keeps us from acquiring a target for our rage and contempt during his Passion, during which he suffered unimaginable torture. Crucifixion was designed to be as painful and as public as possible. Those who were crucified were considered by the state to be the worst of the worst, and the Romans felt that by making examples of enemies of the state, they could take away the appetite for insurrection. Soldiers making it worse than it needed to be only added to the power of dissuasion, so excess was often overlooked, if not encouraged.

But in some early Christian manuscripts,[2] a name is given to at least one of the soldiers responsible for Christ's suffering—Longinus. His name derives from the Greek word *longche*, the name of the long lance used by centurions. It was a weapon of war, not of capital punishment. Using a *longche* was not common for crucifixions, as crucifixions were supposed to take time and leave indelible psychological scars upon those witnessing the death of criminals who challenged state power. But on this day, the religious establishment needed the criminals dead before sundown, before the holy day began. So Longinus dutifully obeyed Pilate, and the religious leaders who petitioned him, in speeding things along. This was not standard operating procedure, but it was still technically a lawful order.

---

1. The asterisk indicates that the soldier saint was martyred for the faith. See introduction to part 2.
2. The first time Longinus appears apart from the Gospels is found in something called "The Acts of Pilate," which claims to be a report from Pilate to the emperor Tiberius. However, since Romans didn't waste time talking about noncitizens they executed, it was probably drafted and circulated by early Christian communities to expand upon the story of Jesus' Passion.

Longinus dutifully administered the deathblow to the two beside Jesus: a club to the legs to hasten suffocation.[3] Unlike the others on their crosses, Jesus was unresponsive and possibly dead. But an order is an order—Longinus had to be sure, so he used the only implement long enough to reach the condemned. As he plunged his spear into Jesus' side, Longinus would have been surprised by the gush of blood and water, evidence that the "insurrectionist" had suffered hypovolemic shock and asphyxiation before he died. The extreme loss of blood had caused water to pool around Jesus' pericardium; meaning Longinus' lance had penetrated the sac surrounding his heart. All in a day's work for the loyal soldier.

"You have bested an enemy; you have come out on top! But in a millisecond, it turns to utter shame—oh my God, what have I done?"

But the day wasn't over yet. The Gospels recount that the sky turned dark and an earthquake shook the land, sending bodies from their graves and tearing in two a massive curtain in the Jewish temple.[4] It was enough to strike fear in the heart of the strongest of men. Longinus must have been terrorized, crying out in fear with the blood-soaked spear in his crimson-hued hand, "Surely this man was the Son of God!"[5] This man that he had made certain was dead by piercing his heart was not one of the many sons of Zeus or Jupiter, but the one God, who had one begotten son, and Longinus had killed him!

3. The cruciform shape of a person awaiting death on a cross would put tremendous pressure on the chest cavity. The nails in their hands and feet, which carried all the weight, likely brushed against major nerves (think root canal without Novocain). Catching one's breath requires expanding the chest, but breathing caused severe pain and quickly exhausted the person. Crushing their legs would speed death, as the person's arms would not have the strength to lift the body in order to breathe.
4. The splitting of the temple curtain is significant a) because it separated the temple courts from the holy of holies that contained the most sacred ark of the covenant, and b) it was about as thick a man's thigh.
5. Matthew 27:54 and Mark 15:39.

In my experience, soldiers tell fellow soldiers stories they don't share with their therapists. Those who talk with me know I share with them the experience of witnessing, and perhaps perpetrating, the killing of other human beings. It rarely comes out in books and articles written about veterans—but it does in the storytelling—that the first emotion a person experiences is elation. You have bested an enemy; you have come out on top! But in a millisecond, it turns to utter shame—oh my God, what have I done?

Longinus almost certainly felt this, as did any of those responsible for Jesus' death, including even Judas, who had knowingly betrayed his friend in exchange for thirty silver coins. He was not present at Golgotha, the place known as Death, but word travels fast. Judas soon learned of Jesus' fate, which he had not anticipated. Oh my God, what have I done? Matthew tells us that Judas was seized with remorse and hanged himself in a place known as the Field of Blood.

Was Longinus any less guilty than Judas? He had contributed directly to the death of this man, the Son of God. Was he not even guiltier than Judas? He held the spear in his blood-soaked hands, he had figuratively been the one left with the smoking gun in his hand! Like Judas, soldiers sometimes recognize the evil they've done and implode, by turning their anger and confusion inward and committing suicide with horrifying frequency.[6] But Jesus calls for a different kind of atonement, a new accounting system for sins. Legend holds that Longinus repented and converted to Christianity, casting his longche aside[7] and leaving the army to be instructed by the apostles. Legend maintains that he was killed for the faith, the first military martyr and a saint. His relics are in Rome, and his lance is within one of four pillars above the altar at St. Peter's Basilica.

6. The two major sources for this information are a CBS investigative report published in 2007 and a 2012 internal review by the Veterans Administration relying on data from 45 states. The former found that over 17 veterans killed themselves every day: http://www.cbsnews.com/stories/2007/11/13/cbsnews_investigates/main3496471.shtml, while the latter found the number to have increased to 22 every day: http://usnews.nbcnews.com/_news/2013/02/01/16811249-22-veterans-commit-suicide-each-day-va-report?lite.

7. Longinus's spear was supposedly recovered centuries later and called "The Holy Lance" or the "Spear of Destiny." It was thought to have special powers (think Indiana Jones–type lore) and was seen as priceless. There are at least four different artifacts supposed to be the spear, one of which is under the dome of Saint Peter's Basilica, where the pope celebrates mass in Rome.

Not long after the coming of the Spirit in Acts 2, the apostle Peter has a very important vision about receiving Gentiles into the new church of which he was the Rock.[1] Up until this vision, the church was mostly made up of Jews who believed Jesus was the Christ, God's Messiah on earth. Greek converts to Judaism were few in number—but now, in the church, the doors were about to swing wide open.

Acts 10 begins by introducing this devout and God-fearing Gentile military man who, instead of taking more than he deserved, gives to those in need and prays often. Before we hear of Peter's vision we learn that Cornelius had a vision of his own. In it, his donations to the poor are called a memorial offering before God. His vision concludes and he sends a few servants, including a subordinate soldier, to Joppa to summon Peter, as he was instructed in his vision. A man of authority knows not just how to dish out orders, but also receive them.

1. This reference comes from Matthew 16:18, where Jesus gives Simon his new name, Peter (in the Greek, *petras*, which means rock) upon which the Lord would build his church.

Nine verses into the chapter, we get to Peter. On a roof in between meals, he falls asleep on an empty stomach (which might explain why God chooses to speak to him through cuisine instead of some other medium). He sees animals that the Bible forbids him to eat, animals that are impure and unclean, and he is told to slaughter and eat them. A voice criticizes him for calling impure that which God has made clean. It happens three times before he wakes up, but it leaves him bewildered. While he is still contemplating this vision, hopefully after he has had a bite to eat, servants sent by Cornelius find him and the Spirit tells Peter to go with them.

"The Spirit sent the gift of discernment through a Gentile named Cornelius. And not just any Gentile, but a Roman military commander."

Somewhere in these events, Peter recognized what the vision was about. The Spirit sent the gift of discernment through a Gentile named Cornelius. And not just any Gentile, but a Roman military commander, many of whom were frequently strangers to Jews at best and active enemies at worst. Soldiers in first century Palestine were the face of the Roman Empire, the most vicious and violent force on earth if they wanted to be. Peter acknowledges to the centurion that it was against his religious law for a Jew to associate with or visit a Gentile. It is this fact that makes the humility of these biblical soldiers so noteworthy, because hubris could easily have been expected from the most advanced and successful military force of that era.

★ ★ ★

Cornelius, this potentially dangerous foreign military commander, held the key to interpreting Peter's vision. Without Cornelius, Peter may not have properly understood what God was telling him. Soldiers today also have a priceless and urgent gift to give the church. We risk misinterpreting our theological and political heritage

if we fail to recognize the presence and perspective of the soldiers in our midst. Some pacifist traditions in particular seem to overlook the fact that soldiers have been a part of our faith from before the birth of the church at Pentecost. But Longinus and Cornelius show that military personnel are part of our biblical foundation—even if these soldiers eventually reevaluated their military roles. Some traditions maintain that Cornelius left the military to become a church elder and eventually the first bishop of Caesarea. Like Longinus before him, he too is a saint.

To most fully be the body that God intends and desires, the church must come to terms with this terrible wisdom our military members have acquired through the fires of hell, the bloody battlefields of Iraq and Afghanistan, Vietnam, Korea, the European and Pacific theaters of World War II, and many more. We must stop valorizing our warriors, but we must also stop vilifying them; we must let them be the human beings they are, capable of good and evil alike.

"We must stop valorizing our warriors, but we must also stop vilifying them; we must let them be the human beings they are, capable of good and evil alike."

Cornelius provided Peter the key to understand God's inclusive vision for the church, an expansive and ambitious vision of growth and diversity. In fact, it is a vision the modern Western church is clamoring for in light of massive declines in membership and vibrancy. But to access this modern key to our faith we must overcome the significant moral and spiritual pain our soldiers and veterans have acquired as a result of years of unjust wars and rumors of war—but also as a result of the deafening silence of churches.

Archangel Michael

Daniel 10 and 12, Jude 1, and Revelation 12

Not all soldier saints enter history and take human form. Michael the archangel is often referred to as the commander of God's armies, but he only appears a few times in the Bible. In each appearance, he commands the heavenly companies; first in Daniel in the prophet's apocalyptic vision in chapters 10 and 12, and then in the New Testament in Jude chapter 1 and Revelation chapter 12. For that reason, he is often depicted artistically in knight's armor, helmet, and wielding a sword.

In Daniel's apocalypse,[1] Michael is the protector of the people of Israel and chief among the angels of heaven. Jude is like John's apocalypse in describing Michael as the commander of angels contending with the devil.[2] As Joshua before him, Michael knows that it is God who is truly in charge, rebuking Satan not in his own name but in the name of the Lord.

---

1. An apocalypse is a genre of writing, whose literal meaning is "revelation," like the book that carries John's name that completes the Christian Bible. Apocalyptic literature often focuses on the dreams and visions of the author, who is usually a prophet or a seer. Its heavy use of metaphor means it is unwise to read it literally. Examples (besides Daniel and Revelation) include parts of Isaiah, Ezekiel, and Zechariah, and, in the New Testament, Matthew 24, parts of Matthew 25, and Mark 13.
2. Jude 1:9; Revelation 12:7.

Due to this imagery, many soldiers throughout church history revered Michael, especially the militant monastic orders that carried out the Crusades, including the Knights Templar and Hospitaller.[3] As an angel, he never dies, but his (and all angels') feast is celebrated by many Western Christians on September 29th. In some Eastern Orthodox churches he is so highly revered that his feast is celebrated on the twelfth of *every* month, in which he has a number of hymns and prayers devoted to him as the defender of both Israel and the church. For Jehovah's Witnesses and Seventh Day Adventists, Michael is another name for Christ, and he is thought to prefigure Jesus in the Old Testament.

"Michael the archangel is a complex figure, as is any soldier."

But before he became more associated with military vestments and endeavors, early Christians saw Michael's protective traits as those of a healer. Emperor Constantine, who ended the persecution of Christians with the Edict of Milan in 313, constructed the earliest Christian shrine to Michael. His Michaelion church was in modern day Chalcedon near a site known for its healing waters. When Constantine defeated his foe Licinius in 324, however, he depicted Michael as a warrior defeating a large serpent. The image of a soldier running his lance through a dragon stuck for ages, but not before at least one significant hurrah in favor of healing. In the sixth century, Pope Gregory prayed for an end to a great sickness plaguing Rome, and the archangel appeared over a mausoleum, sword in hand. In recognition, the pope renamed the site *Castel Sant'angelo*; Castle of the Holy Angel.

Michael the archangel is a complex figure, as is any soldier. He is both protector and enforcer. The unnamed angel who appears to Joshua

3. The Knights Hospitaller are not to be confused with the Brothers Hospitallers, which will come up later.

Archangel Michael

I am
an
American
Soldier
for 20 years and a
Christian for 14.
... the same God
of peace
is also a God of War
that defends the helpless
and brings evil
into His light
You might see that WE
the Military
are the tool of God
for His right and just purpose and that Our flags do have a place in a Christian store.
God gave freedom but it must be defended with blood, sweat and tears
and WE are America's lambs .

before the battle of Jericho is often assumed to be Michael, which makes sense, as "the commander of the Lord's army." Some have also suggested that it is Michael who is "the angel of the Lord" of 1 Chronicles 21, who pursues David after Satan incites the king to take a census of the people of Israel. Michael does not fit easily into our compartments of either pacifist or patriot. But we can say that he is a righteous commander of the Lord; he does not take orders from human beings but looks to God for guidance.

★ ★ ★

The Hebrew name Michael means "who is like God?"—a rhetorical question. Nobody is like God. The name therefore has come to confer humility upon those so named. Perhaps it is fitting, then, that Michael is the patron of soldiers and warriors, since humility is often a common characteristic in godly warriors. Indeed, who is like God? "Who is like the Lord our God," asks Psalm 113, "the One who sits enthroned on high, who stoops down to look on the heavens and the earth?"[4]

"If humility is not above our God, far be it from us not to be humble."

Some pacifists observe that taking human life is like acting as judge, jury, and executioner. If Michael reminds us of anything, perhaps it is that in the immense moral complexity of soldiering, it is not for us to judge those who participate in warcraft because of their conviction that they are honoring God or bringing about a greater good. Some have healed, some have harmed. Some have blessed, some have bled. When the angel of the Lord spared David's life, he fell on his face, shouldered the blame, and begged for mercy.[5] If humility is not above our God, far be it from us not to be humble. May God bring healing, and have mercy on all of us, sinners and saints alike.

4. Psalm 113:4-5.
5. 1 Chronicles 21:8, 17.

Part II

Soldier Saints

After the first century in the Common Era (CE), Christian believers were left with the Holy Spirit and one another to live the life of faith Jesus paved for them. The model for their lives was Jesus, who was confronted by the powers that be, unjustly accused, and killed for humanity's sake. Therefore, being similarly persecuted and killed for the faith was a normal path for many early Christians. The Greek word for bearing witness was *martus*, or martyr, and martyrdom was seen as the ultimate display of faith. Polycarp of Smyrna, an early bishop discipled by the apostle John, went rejoicing to the Coliseum to be eaten by beasts, for he felt it would be the greatest honor to die persecuted, as Christ himself was. Many other Christians were to follow him. The martyrs showed with their lives and by their deaths that they heard, believed, and obeyed Jesus. Martyrdom was sometimes called "the crown of faith."

As the faith grew and spread, the place of Roman officials and soldiers converting to Christianity began to be discussed in the church. Until then statecraft had seemed to be in the business of killing Christians; were these supposed saints really just spies in disguise? One of the most peace-oriented early theologians before the political shifts set in motion by Emperor Constantine I in the fourth century was Tertullian, who wrote about a disciple of his, one of the earliest accounts of these converted soldiers. His student did not leave the military as was most common among converts, but instead displayed his faith by refusing to wear a wreath of laurels on his head in a military parade. His peers accused him of insubordination and he suffered for his faith, gaining instead for himself the "crown" of martyrdom.[1]

The people featured in the following pages all had intimate familiarity with the military of their day, either for having served or refused service in some way. Many of them were killed for refusing either to

1. Tertullian writes of this disciple in his 211 CE treatise *De corona milites* (On the Soldier's Crown). In it, he uses a lot of plays on words, since the early church referred to themselves metaphorically as *militia Christi*, the army of Christ. This book relies on similar rhetorical gymnastics to draw attention to the same line that our forebears saw so sharply.

worship their head of state or to commit state-sanctioned violence. All of them have been canonized in various Christian traditions, earning the title "saint."[2] But this word is confusing, since in the Bible it refers to all believers. Some traditions, especially Roman Catholic, Eastern Orthodox, and a few Protestant denominations, however, recognize that some of the saints embody a particularly holy life deserving of extra acclaim. Canonization is the process through which a believer becomes recognized as a saint—and it is from these canonized saints that we draw for the profiles in this section.

For those soldier saints I have included—only several among many—I reference their feast day where I can, deferring to the Western church's liturgical calendar when necessary. The dates that they lived are often an approximation, indicated by a "ca." for *circa*, Latin for "approximately." Finally, the historicity of each saint varies. Some are almost certainly legend, sometimes the result of a few local heroes being combined into one legendary figure whom the community memorializes. As with any story of great age, the literal truth of a story is less important than the figurative truth contained in it. All of these stories were passed down by Christians of various ages and had measureable impact on communities who took care to transmit them. Their value is found not in whether they literally occurred, but what they do to shape us in the here and now. These soldiers are saints not for their own glory, but for ours, so that in reflecting upon them we may come to reflect the holiness in them. For that reason, I include a short prayer at the end of each of these profiles. In the traditions mentioned above, praying with the saints is a common practice, and where possible, I have tried to preserve popular short prayers, called novenas, that I have come across in my study of these holy men and women.

---

2. Traditions that recognize saints are Eastern and Oriental Orthodox, Roman Catholic, Lutheran, and Anglican/Episcopal church bodies. While a few are pretty standard, like the apostles and figures from the early church, different traditions frequently recognize particular saints that others do not. For example, Orthodox churches are the only ones to venerate Constantine I, while those in the Anglican communion revere Thomas Cranmer, the author of the *Book of Common Prayer*.

As I hope you will see as you reflect on these lives, the martial fraternity represents a kind of alternative interpretive community, one with a particular perspective on faith and warcraft. We catch things that others sometimes overlook, and our perspective can be a gift to the church. One thing that we can provide the church is the witness of lives lived for a good greater than self. One of the distinctive marks of a soldier is that they stand prepared to forfeit their entire lives, the epitome of self-sacrifice. When you see an asterisk in the profile's title, it indicates that the soldier saint was martyred for the faith. If you want to dig deeper into this particular community within the church, appendix 9 has a list of these and many more soldier saints arranged by the date they died, and the bibliography offers more literary sources on these and other soldier saints of note.

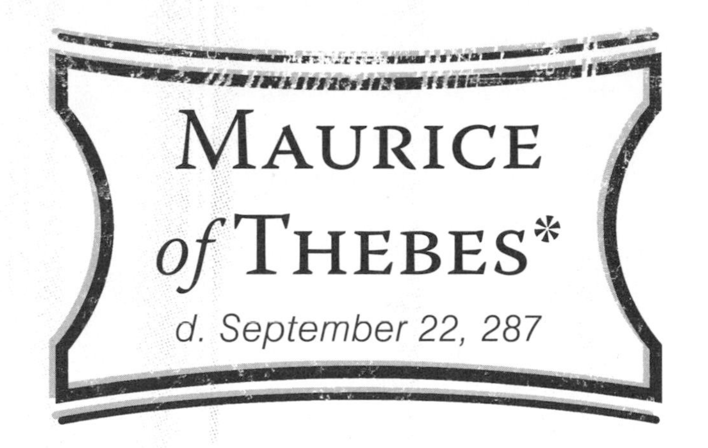

Maurice of Thebes*

d. September 22, 287

The Holy Lance (sometimes called the Spear of Destiny) supposedly was passed from Saint Longinus all the way to Maurice of Thebes (Luxor, Egypt), a Christian officer who commanded a large Roman legion made up of 6,666 soldiers. Emperor Maximian commanded Maurice to march from Egypt to France to help quell a violent rebellion by the Burgundy people in Gaul. Maurice willingly obeyed, recognizing that the sword was wielded by the Roman authority to ensure justice. As they crossed the Swiss Alps and neared their destination, however, they were ordered to attack a group of Christians. Maurice wrote to his commander:

> Emperor, we are your soldiers but also the soldiers of the true God. We owe you military service and obedience, but we cannot renounce Him who is our Creator and Master, and also yours even though you reject Him. In all things which are not against His law, we most willingly obey you, as we have done hitherto. We readily oppose your enemies whoever they are, but we cannot stain our hands with the blood of innocent people [Christians]. We have taken an oath to God before we took one to you, you cannot place any confidence in our second oath if we violate the other [the first]. You commanded us to execute Christians, behold we are such.[1]

1. http://www.coptic.net/synexarion/MauriceOfTheba.txt, retrieved May 21, 2013. Another important resource is David Woods's page on Maurice; http://www.ucc.ie/milmart/Maurice.html.

Indeed, legend holds that all 6,666 soldiers under Maurice were Christian. Under Maurice's encouragement, every man refused this patently unjust order. For their supposed insubordination, the emperor had the legion decimated (from Latin *decimus*, meaning "tenth"), ordering another unit to execute every tenth soldier of the Theban Legion. After watching their comrades be killed, the men remained loyal to Maurice and still would not obey the Caesar, so Maximian again ordered every tenth man killed. This continued until there was none left to kill. All 6,666 Christian soldiers were killed by order of the emperor for refusing to obey.

One of the last men slain, Maurice insisted:

> We confess God the Father the creator of all things and His Son Jesus Christ, God. We have seen our comrades slain with the sword, we do not weep for them but rather rejoice at their honor. Neither this, nor any other provocation has tempted us to revolt. Behold, we have arms in our hands, but we do not resist, because we would rather die innocent than live by any sin.

Though Maurice and his men were armed, they did not revolt, but willingly submitted themselves to unjust punishment for refusing to commit violence against fellow Christians.[2]

Because Christianity was openly persecuted until into the fourth century, the idea of having thousands of openly professing Christians in a legion is probably exaggerated. In other words, the legend of the Theban legion is not historically accurate. Regardless, the legend persisted and continued to hold sway in Christian communities for centuries. The Abbey of Saint Maurice-en-Valais was dedicated in 515 CE on the site of the supposed decimation. To this day the abbey holds many relics of the soldier saints said to have been killed, including Maurice's lieutenants: Exupernis, Candidus, and Innocent. The oldest images of Maurice depict him as a black African, which is likely to be true of a number of his compatriots, who have been the patrons of black soldiers especially.

Maurice himself, killed at the hand of his own commander in chief, ironically remains today the patron saint of armies and the infantry in particular. In fact, the United States National Infantry Association awards the Order of Saint Maurice to soldiers who "have served the Infantry community with distinction; demonstrated a significant contribution in support of the Infantry; and represent the highest standards of integrity, moral character, professional competence, and dedication to duty."[3] Replace *infantry* with *church* and Maurice might heartily approve.

---

2. Many years ago, Mennonite Central Committee produced a poster suggesting "A Modest Proposal for Peace," that the Christians of the world stop killing one another. This begged the question whether Christians should be killing *anyone*, but refusing to kill our brothers and sisters in Christ was a start. It took Maurice's principle and applied it to the persistent violence among Christians that would follow Constantine's time, when officially "Christian" nations vied for power and took up arms against each other. Duke University theologian Stanley Hauerwas keeps the poster on his office door. Passersby often comment that it seems self-righteous for Christians to refuse to kill only their own. "But," he insists, "we have to start somewhere." He also writes about the Modest Proposal for Peace in his book with Jean Vanier: *Living Gently in a Violent World* (Downers Grove, IL: InterVarsity, 2008).
3. http://www.infantryassn.com/pages/awards.html.

VALIENT STEADFAST

★ ★ ★

Lord God almighty, Maurice and his legion fought valiantly on the battlefield of faith, steadfastly opposed the tyranny of earthly rulers, boldly confessed faith in the one true God, and preferred to die by the sword rather than to betray our Lord, Jesus Christ. A holy martyr and loyal soldier of Christ, Maurice's legend displayed for us the courage to persevere in truth, to be a light in the darkness of the times in which we live. God, give your legion, the church, the grace to endure patiently all the trials and hardships of this life, and to carry our cross in the spirit of prayer and self-denial, through Christ our Lord. Amen.[4] ☧

4. Adapted from http://www.stmauricechurch.com/about.html, retrieved May 21, 2013.

Sebastian of Milan**[1]

ca. 256–January 20, 288

Emperors Diocletian and Maximian ruled the western part of the Roman Empire in the late third century during many persecutions against the church. A large number of Christians were martyred, especially in offices of public service, like officers in the military. Public servants were expected to be loyal to the emperor to the point of death, just as many modern soldiers swear oaths of allegiance. Christians, however, were intent on obeying the biblical prohibitions against swearing oaths[2] and worshiping other gods. Refusing to worship a head of state was a capital crime.

> *"Christian 'atheism' was a threat to national security."*

Sebastian knew Maximian and Diocletian personally from his top post in the Praetorian Guard, the unit assigned to protect the emperors over the years. By all accounts, he was indoctrinated in Milan, Italy,

---

1. Two asterisks here indicate that Sebastian was martyred twice—once left for dead, and then killed.
2. Matthew 5:33-35; James 5:12.

and became a Christian after entering the military as a captain in the emperors' bodyguard detail. Not for his own sake, but for the stability of the empire he served the emperors to the best of his ability (though his religion was a secret to them). He did this fully aware of the empire's persecution of Christians. While protecting the life of the caesars, he covertly encouraged the secret faith of many Christians facing persecution. He never renounced his role in the Praetorian Guard, instead perhaps using his social position to garner resources or pacify the worst of the persecutions for his fellow Christians. However, before long, his faith was found out and fellow soldiers loyal to Maximian questioned him vigorously.

Sebastian was accused of atheism, since he refused to worship the Roman gods. A widespread belief was that mass punishment was the gods' favored response to impiety. Christian "atheism" was, therefore, a threat to national security. But Sebastian replied, "Always I have worshiped Jesus Christ for [the emperor's] health and for the state of Rome, and I think for to pray and demand help of the idols of stone is a great folly." Indeed, he felt that worshiping the state idols did Diocletian harm, and to pray to Christ for his health was of greater benefit. Why err by worshiping stone, when we can petition the Son of God for the health of Rome? This didn't satisfy the inquisitors, and Sebastian was sentenced to death by being shot full of arrows. He was taken outside the city, tied to a tree and the local law enforcement officers did their duty and eventually left poor Sebastian for dead.

"Why err by worshiping stone, when we can petition the Son of God for the health of Rome?"

But Sebastian wasn't finished yet. Irene, a Christian in Rome, discovered that he still had breath in him, and nursed the soldier back to health. Unable to restrain himself, and not willing to live in secret (and in peace) by taking advantage of his miraculously gained second life, Sebastian sought out his former employer, Caesar, and found him amidst a parade in the sovereign's honor. When the emperor came within earshot, Sebastian cried out with all he had, showing by his presence that God did, and would, have the last word. From his perch he shouted:

> The bishops of the idols deceive you evilly which accuse the Christian men to be contrary to the common profit of the city, that pray for your estate and for the health of Rome. . . . Therefore our Lord hath rendered to me life to the end that I should tell you that evilly and cruelly you persecute Christians.[3]

Still with the interest of the city in mind, Sebastian insisted that the emperor's court clerics, who falsely accused Christians of being isolationists and waiting the fall of Rome, were liars. No, he claimed, Christians have the health of their city at heart, possibly remembering Jeremiah's similar call to seek the welfare of the city.[4] In fact, he credited his pseudoresurrection to Jesus wanting him to tell the emperor

3. http://www.catholic-saints.net/saints/st-sebastian.php, retrieved May 21, 2013.
4. Jeremiah 29:7.

that his persecutions of Christians were cruel and evil, and targeted people who were not against the state but in favor of its peace and prosperity.[5] Diocletian didn't seem to like this message, so he ordered Sebastian beaten to death, this time for good.

Sebastian is known as the saint who was martyred twice, once with arrows and again with the club, both by soldiers serving their emperor dutifully. Ironically, he became one of their own patron saints.

★ ★ ★

Heavenly Commander, your servant Sebastian chose to be a soldier of Christ and dared to spread faith in the King of kings, even as he knew of the persecution of his brothers and sisters in faith. In a world of systemic injustice in which we ourselves often bear indirect complicity in evil, Sebastian gives us an example by which to live our lives despite the ever-present burden of sin. Lord, give us the eyes to see and ears to hear the painful truth of the church's sins of commission and omission, to acknowledge the sinner and saint in each of us and in our neighbor. Give us the faith to be still when you whisper reassuringly but responsive when you beckon urgently, through your son, our Savior, Jesus Christ. Amen.

5. This was the call of Jeremiah 29:7 to Israel in another, earlier, empire—Babylon.

Maximilian *of* Tebessa*

274–October 30, 295

Nearing the fourth century, Roman citizenship and military service were not as closely tied as they once had been. It used to be that in order to serve in the Roman Senate, a man had to have served a full term in the military (sometimes as long as twenty-five years). But now Rome had changed, and the Senate had very few veterans in their ranks. Conscription was the rule of the day, and large swaths of young men in the farthest reaches of the provinces were swept up and drafted in.

Maximilian grew up in such an area, far away from the center of the empire, in Tebessa (now a part of Algeria, in northern Africa). When he was twenty-one, the draft blew through his hometown. Maximilian's father, Victor, took him to be measured for a soldier's

uniform, as was custom for those conscripted into the military. At this time, recruits would be given lead pieces something like a set of dog tags. Life in the military was glorious and daring, and many young men, even Christians, would relish the opportunity for fun, travel, and adventure. But not Maximilian; he had been baptized not long before his birthday. Entering the church was not fun and adventurous, but demanding and dangerous. The training required for confirmation and baptism was a grueling ordeal that included fasting and carried with it grave risk.

"Before 312 CE, Christianity was illegal, and many Christians were executed as enemies of the state."

Before 312 CE, Christianity was illegal, and many Christians were executed as enemies of the state. Because they called one another "brother" and "sister," yet somehow produced children, they were accused of incest. Because they ate the "body" of Jesus when they took communion, they were accused of cannibalism and practicing magic (since before they ate the body it was mere bread). Maximilian was a Christian. He could tolerate false accusations of incest, cannibalism, and magic, but he could not see himself being a soldier. His identity was rooted not in Romulus and Remus, but the man named Jesus.

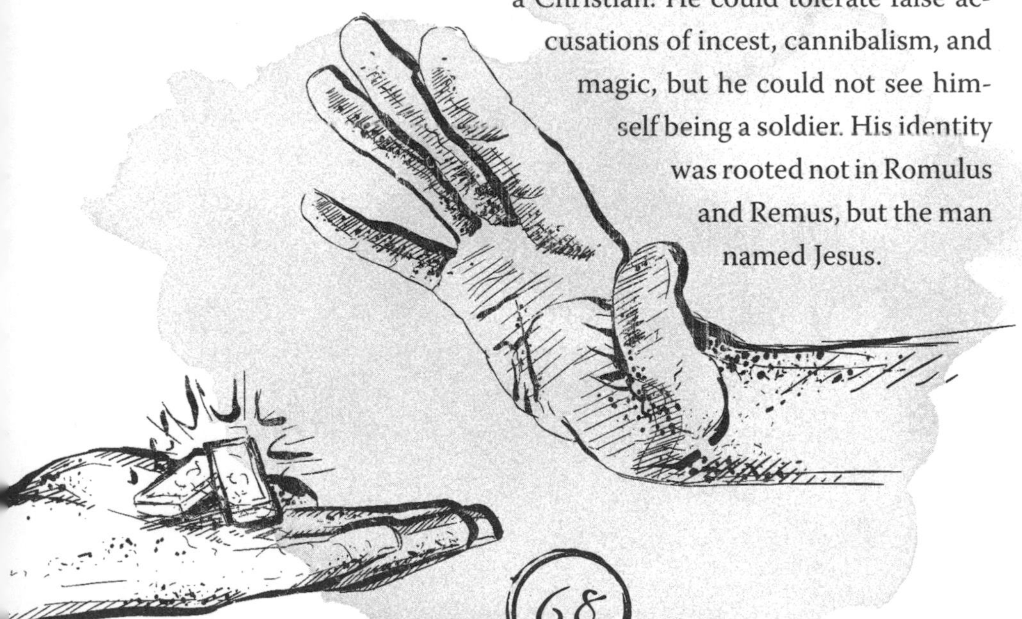

"My service is for my Lord; I cannot serve the world."

Led before the local recruiter to have his measurements taken, Maximilian insisted that military service was at odds with his being a Christian. "I cannot serve in the military; I cannot do wrong; I am a Christian."[1] He asked why his name was being recorded and refused to accept his dog tags, which he called "the world's seal," since he had already accepted "the saving seal of my Lord Jesus Christ, the Son of the Living God." The officials reminded him that other Christians saw no problem with serving in the army, that many virile young men positively enjoyed the life of a soldier. Maximilian begged to differ, saying; "My service is for my Lord; I cannot serve the world. I have already said: I cannot serve in the military; I cannot do wrong; I am a Christian." Maximilian's identity complex certainly confused the draft board: why on earth would this young man choose death over the playboy lifestyle of the few, the proud—the Roman legions? Threatened with death, Maximilian insisted that he could not die: "Even if I do depart the world, my spirit will live with my Lord Christ." Sure enough, his name was crossed off the draft record and his discharge read: "Disloyally refused the military oath and service."

Conscientious objection in his day was a capital crime, and Maximilian was then and there sentenced to die by the very sword he refused to carry. His father, Victor, watched as he gave thanks to God for the medal of honor he would receive, the crown of martyrdom. Before insisting to his father that his clothes be given to the guard preparing to execute him, he encouraged other secret (and not so secret) Christians: "With an eager desire, hurry with as much courage as you can so that it may befall you to see the Lord and that he may reward you also with a similar crown." With that, he was "crowned" a martyr.

1. All quotes here are drawn from David Woods's interpretation at http://www.ucc.ie/milmart/Maximilian.html, retrieved May 21, 2013.

Both of my parents were in the army ,
my dad was in combat as part of the 82nd airborne,
both of my grandfathers were in the army.
all have wanted to do was carry on
the military tradition of my family .

. . . I don't want to anymore and I'm scared to tell anyone . . .
I feel like i've made a huge mistake.

. . . I really feel like God is calling me to do something else with my life. . .
i don't know if there even is a way to get out of it at this point
. . . All I know to do right now is put my trust in God,
which is the best i think i can do.

His final statement was intended not just for those Christians within earshot, but for any of us with an ear to history. Maximilian knew that his identity was imprinted in Christ, not found on the information stamped onto a set of dog tags. No seal this world might have us wear determines who and whose we are, as we bear the saving seal of the Lord Jesus Christ, our true commander in chief.

★ ★ ★

God above, your servant Maximilian was a man of profound conviction who saw his identity in your son, Jesus Christ, very clearly, even to the point of death by the sword he was asked to carry. Give us, your people, a similar sense of conviction, of where and when and why to say to the world, with our brother Maximilian, "I cannot do wrong, I am a Christian." Though we may be diverse in those things which we cannot compromise, guide us to be one in your Son Jesus, in answer to his prayer for us. Likewise, give us a courageous zeal for your glory, in answer to Maximilian's appeal, through Christ our Lord. Amen. ☧

Marcellus *of* Tangier*

ca. 250–October 30, 298

In the Roman Empire during the first few centuries of the church, the head of state was worshiped as a son of the gods and savior of Rome. The day a man became Caesar was an annual day of celebration and worship. This presented problems for Christians, who worshiped Jesus of Nazareth as the Son of the true God and as Savior. Many early Christians in public service were confronted by these dual allegiances and could not reconcile worshiping two masters, Jesus and Caesar. The emperor held the sword, and often wielded it against those who refused to worship him, the most powerful man of the civilized world. Marcellus was one such man in public service in the Roman military.[1]

On July 21, 298, he was part of a planned parade in Tangier for Caesar's "birthday," which marked the day Maximian had ascended from mere humanity to become the divine emperor. Marcellus, who had most

1. The primary source for Marcellus's life is translated by David Woods at http://www.ucc.ie/milmart/Marcellus.html. It is also the source for a play written by the Orthodox Peace Fellowship and performed live on Marcellus's feast day, October 30th, by the Catholic Peace Fellowship. Talk about an ecumenical experience! You can read the script based on Woods's translation at http://www.incommunion.org/2007/10/27/saint-marcellus-military-martyr.

likely been baptized after his conscription,[2] knew his allegiance was to a higher power than Caesar. Before Maximian's entourage reached the place where Marcellus was standing, he threw down his weapon and military uniform and proclaimed loudly:

> I serve Jesus Christ the Eternal King. Henceforward I cease to serve your Emperors, and I scorn to worship your gods of wood and stone, which are deaf and dumb idols. If such be the terms of service that men are forced to offer sacrifice to gods and Emperors, behold I cast away my vine-switch and belt, I renounce the standards, and refuse to serve.[3]

He was willing to serve the civic authority only if his enlistment did not require sacrifice to false gods, like the emperor. Unfortunately, Rome had no qualms with requiring its public servants to worship the state system in place. Marcellus was apprehended in the midst of the imperial parade and imprisoned on the charge of sedition and insanity. When he was questioned later about the charges, he reaffirmed:

> I am a Christian and cannot serve under this allegiance, but only under the allegiance of Jesus Christ the Son of God the Father Almighty. [I cast away my arms,] for it is not right for a Christian, who serves the Lord Christ, to serve the cares of the world.[4]

---

2. The early church refused communion to those Christians who considered enlisting after they had been baptized, since they were seen as despising God in favor of the emperor. But soldiers who converted after they enlisted or were conscripted were allowed to remain in the military if they refused orders to kill.
3. "Saint Marcellus: Military Martyr." *In Communion*. Orthodox Peace Fellowship, 27 Oct. 2007, http://www.incommunion.org/2007/10/27/saint-marcellus-military-martyr, accessed May 21, 2013. Roman officers carried branches as a sign of their rank, but also as tools to slap subordinates. Their belts also were indicators of rank and prestige. Standards were like unit guidons; they were carried in parades and in battle to signify Roman power and often also had features unique to individual units. But they were also much more than that, symbolizing the presence of the gods. The quotation is taken from a play based on Marcellus's passion (http://www.ucc.ie/milmart/Marcellus.html), read every year at the University of Notre Dame by the Catholic Peace Fellowship as part of their annual Marcellus Award ceremony. See http://www.incommunion.org/2007/10/27/saint-marcellus-military-martyr for more info.
4. Anne Fremantle, ed., *A Treasury of Early Christianity* (New York: Viking Press, 1953), pp. 233–236.

TESTIMONY

Not only would he not worship a false god, he found that his duty to the state and his duty to God stood in opposition to one another. He did not deny that he broke the law; he was guilty as charged, at least as far as the state was concerned. On the dual charge of sedition and insanity, he was imprisoned for three months, from the day he objected on July 21 to October 30, when he was questioned again and beheaded, after reaffirming his "insane remarks."[5] Cassian, the stenographer recording the proceedings of the kangaroo court, was so moved by Marcellus's testimony that he refused to go on transcribing the trial, and was beheaded not long after the seditious centurion met his own fate. Interestingly, the next person to fill the office of pope (in 308) took the name Marcellus, almost certainly aware of the soldier saint bearing the same name who was killed just ten years prior.

★ ★ ★

Roman Catholic and Orthodox Christians remember the saints in many ways; composing prayers in their memory, painting icons of their likeness, and beautifying their gravesites and bodily remains. Bodily remains and other objects belonging to the saints are

5. Part of his passion includes his peers accusing him of being insane. The abrupt and sensational nature of his actions certainly did not help him.

known as relics, and they are treated with the same respect one would give the saint himself or herself. Ironically, Marcellus's relics now rest beneath the altar of a university that bears the motto "God, Country, Notre Dame." Every year, the Catholic Peace Fellowship, based near the University of Notre Dame, performs a play based on Marcellus's passion and issues an award to a person of faith and conscience, in recognition of Marcellus's profound witness. The university has a healthy and robust military Reserve Officer Training Corps (ROTC), though the saint who watches over the basilica in Indiana may have had something colorful to say about the second part of their motto. Sometimes our memory needs to be jogged, and we can give thanks both for the cadets and cadre who train to protect their country as well as the prophetic witness of peace fellowships and soldier saints.

★ ★ ★

God of all ages, who was, is, and will ever be; give us the patience to bear witness to the example of your servant Marcellus, who challenges us to be aware of how we celebrate our citizenship. Keep us aware that carrying swords and standards can at times prevent us from carrying our crosses. Though we may ask it, we need not more arms, but more contrite hearts, tuned to your will and reflective of your ways. Bear with us in mercy amidst those times in which our convictions set us in opposition to our own governments, and bless those who carry out their earthly duties despite your heavenly will, as you blessed us while we were your enemy, through Jesus Christ our Lord. Amen. ☧

"Bear with us in mercy and bless those who carry out their earthly duties despite your heavenly will, as you blessed us while we were your enemy."

George*

ca. 280–April 23, 303

George is known the world over as a Christian knight who slayed a dragon. As the story is told, a terrible dragon was terrorizing the city of Sylene, in the modern North African nation of Libya. In exchange for relative calm, the townspeople were offering a sacrifice to the beast at its demand. As George galloped into town, the latest victim would be a beautiful but helpless princess. Rushing in for the rescue, George suppressed the dragon and eventually slayed it in the town after all the inhabitants promised to be baptized.

This story had tremendous appeal during the medieval period, amidst all the chivalric forms of Christianity (and imperial powers) that ruled that age. It is little surprise to learn that George was and is the patron of soldiers and knights. He is also patron saint of England, itself once a vast empire. The knightly stuff seems less relevant to us; like dragon tales, few knights in armor on horses remain in existence today. Besides, George lived and died long before the time of knights. Soldiers, however, still exist in abundance, and George's relevancy to them lies in a tale not so tall.

Some stories hold that George was born into a wealthy family, which would explain his association later with knights and noblemen. He even refers to himself as "a gentleman, a knight of Cappadocia." However, he "left all for to serve the God of heaven;" he gave away all of his worldly wealth before appearing before the "dragon" of the

imperial governors (as some legends have it, Diocletian himself).[1]

The story of the dragon has been thoroughly debunked as embellishment dating to the Middle Ages, when tales of dragons and damsels in distress were more in vogue.[2] Many accounts of George's martyrdom exist, but the dragon appears only in those dated after the twelfth century. The dragon George slays may only have been as real as the dragon John saw in his vision in the book of Revelation. The dragon is a powerful metaphor, a symbol used to point to something else. The earliest depictions of the dragon seem to symbolize Roman governors, who insisted George confess Apollo, god of the sun, as "Lord and Savior of All." Other writers level their pens at Diocletian more personally, as the emperor under whom George would have been serving at the time of his death in 303.

Different hagiographies point to other things that the dragon might represent, such as paganism, or the devil, or perhaps the sins of pride and arrogance. It is clear the ferocious dragon had tremendous power over people, much like the power that nations, states, and empires have and continue to wield.

---

1. David Woods's resources on George are exemplary and very helpful: http://www.ucc.ie/milmart/George.html.
2. One place where you can find the story about the dragon is *The Golden Legend*, a lengthy hagiography written during the medieval period in which the tales of George were so popular. However, many of the tales included went well beyond the narratives that Christian communities were passing down organically. It is hard to tell fiction from fantasy in its pages, though still a useful and illuminating manuscript.

"Funny how soldiers themselves seem to get in the way of the glamorous tales we insist their lives tell."

We know that George was raised by his Palestinian Christian mother and became a soldier in the imperial army. He was martyred near Nicomedia, the eastern Roman capital ruled by Diocletian. George is said to have been tortured many times for criticizing the emperor,[3] each time being resuscitated in order to endure another round of increasingly inventive ways of inflicting extreme pain. In no particular order, he is lacerated by a wheel of swords, consumed by fire, beheaded, chopped into small pieces, and finally buried at different parts of the city. Take your pick of which death he suffered was worst. At any rate, George was killed by the powers that be, even though a few mighty powers claim him as their patron, including England, Portugal, and Germany. Funny how soldiers themselves seem to get in the way of the glamorous tales we insist their lives tell.

★ ★ ★

God of all kingdoms and nations, we give thanks for George, the heroic soldier and defender of your faith, who dared to criticize a tyrannical emperor and was subjected to horrible cruelty. May he be for all time a witness against torture and selfish ambition, for he could have occupied a high military position but preferred to die for you Lord, our God. Give us, your one holy and apostolic church, the great grace of heroic Christian bravery that should mark soldiers of Christ, in the name of your Son, Jesus. Amen.[4]

3. Being critical of one's head of state is never advisable, though sometimes legal. For US service members, the line can be hard to discern. For more information, consult Department of Defense Directive 1325.6, "Handling Dissident and Protest Activities Among Members of the Armed Forces." You can access a PDF of the directive at http://www.dtic.mil/whs/directives/corres/pdf/132506p.pdf.
4. Adapted from http://st-george-medal.com/St-George-Prayer.htm, accessed May 21, 2013.

FLORIAN*

d. May 4, 303

In the middle of the third century, in what is now Austria, a young man was born who would become the patron saint of firefighters.[1] Florian, as he was known, would join the Roman military voluntarily, which was rare for a person so far from central Rome, in the frontier provinces. He was highly regarded for his service up until the turn of the century, when Emperor Diocletian imposed his infamous persecution of Christians in government positions. By that time, Florian had become the commander of the armies around the region of Noricum, where he grew up.

During that time, there was no such thing as a police officer or a firefighter. If you wanted to volunteer to protect and defend, you had to do so with a sword in your hand, not a hose, and a seal around your neck, not a badge upon your breast. Soldiers were the only protectors

1. David Woods's site has many excellent resources on Florian at http://www.ucc.ie/milmart/Florianus.html.

and rescuers. Today our society seems to give greater honor to our military personnel who serve in foreign lands than to our police officers and firefighters who wish to serve the common good domestically. Many young men and women have told me, with sincerity, that to "protect the innocent" or "serve my country" logically requires *military* service. But "the innocent" are also in towns and cities across our own land. Our own country has internal needs that are as worthy and necessary as the needs of other nations.

After a huge fire in Rome the duties of Roman soldiers expanded from protecting the borders to the responsibility of protecting homes and property against fire. By Florian's time, firefighting was a duty expected of military units, and he was so expert at combating fires that he was never seen without his emblematic pitcher of water.[2] However, Diocletian feared that Christians refusing to worship the Roman gods would turn their disfavor upon him and the empire he ruled. In order to regain the favor of the gods, he tried to force the supposedly impious Christians to worship the same gods the rest of the empire did. Like other high-ranking government employees at the time, Florian was expected to worship false gods in order to appease his commander in chief, who himself was referred to in divine terms. His military service, however, did not trump his Christian faith. When he heard that Diocletian's messenger, a man named Aquilius, was in town, Florian wasted no time seeking him out and volunteering once again, this time to suffer the same fate of his Christian brothers and sisters who were being persecuted for their faith.

"I have suffered many wounds for our emperor; now it has come time for me to suffer wounds for the God that I worship."

2. Florian is associated with the establishment of firefighting as another form of service to the state. See appendix 5.

Standing before Aquilius, Florian said "I have suffered many wounds for our emperor; now it has come time for me to suffer wounds for the God that I worship."[3] Aquilius, ever the negotiator, offered Florian a promotion in rank, increased pay, and other bribes. But again, Florian insisted that he be treated no different than other Christians. He went on to be tortured by beatings, he was nearly flayed, and finally he was put on a stake to be burned. Despite his injuries, Florian called out in a loud voice, daring Aquilius to set the pyre alight, that his mastery of the flame was such that he would be carried to heaven upon its tips without being harmed. Aquilius didn't want to be publicly humiliated, so he tied a rope around Florian's neck and threw him in a river instead. The same waters of baptism that gave Florian spiritual life would also be his carriage to heaven.

★ ★ ★

Dear God, through the witness and example of Florian, keep us mindful of our comrades who have died in the performance of their duty. Thank you for all who have gone before us, having given years of their lives to the fulfillment of their responsibilities, which now rest on us. Help us to always remember those who perform extraordinary duties in service to a common good that we share with our fellow citizens and give us grace to prepare each day for our own summons to your tribunal of justice. Amen.[4] ☧

3. Adapted from http://www.stflos.org/Patron%20Saint.html, retrieved May 21, 2013.
4. Adapted from http://www.st-florian-medal.com/st-florian-prayer.htm, retrieved May 21, 2013.

Sergius* and Bacchus*

d. October 7, 303

Many soldiers are known not just for their bravery, but for their commitment to others, especially those who fight alongside them in battle. A common refrain in modern armies is that infantrymen do not fight for much else than "the man or woman on your right and your left." Within one's unit, it is common to find another person to whom one connects more deeply than others, one's "battle buddy." The camaraderie of soldiers is a long tradition that includes the Roman era.

Sergius and Bacchus were as close as David and Jonathan in the Bible. They served under Emperor Galerius in the imperial security force, the Praetorian Guard.[1] Like many other soldier saints, they were likely converted only after they became soldiers. For Christians to serve in the military, which often carried out the executions of Christians, they were required to do so "in the closet," so to speak. Furthermore, only the best soldiers rose in the ranks to the Praetorium, so for Christian

1. David Woods has a lot of great material on Sergius and Bacchus on his website, http://www.ucc.ie/milmart/Sergius.html.

soldiers like Sergius and Bacchus, their esteem was gained by keeping their Christian life secret.

Their prestigious reputation came crashing down, however, one day when the emperor's court was visiting a pagan shrine. At the entrance, the two soldiers stalled, knowing they would be expected to worship false gods should they follow their peers inside. Tragically, their hesitation did not go unnoticed, and they were told to come and make sacrifice. When they partnered together in refusing, they were outed as secret Christians and were subjected to ridicule and derision. A favorite tactic of the emperor was to parade disgraced soldiers in women's clothes. Sergius and Bacchus were not deterred, however, and steadfastly insisted upon their loyalty to God. Seeing their determination, the emperor had them beaten severely. The abuse was so harsh that Bacchus perished while reciting the 23rd Psalm, calling on God to "lead [him] beside still waters . . . in the valley of the shadow of death." Sergius was not so lucky. Bacchus is said to have appeared to him to encourage him in the faith and to persevere, forever a faithful battle buddy. For days, Sergius remained faithful, despite such tortures as having to run eighteen miles in shoes of nails, before finally being beheaded in Syria, where there is a church dedicated to him.

Much has been said about the close relationship of these two saints. Like David and Jonathan before them, speculation runs wild that their union represented the earliest gay Christian couple. Of that we cannot be certain, but what we can be sure of is that their close trust made possible their uniform insistence that they were followers of Christ. Their partnership is not uncommon in the heritage of soldier saints, and several other pairs are worthy of examination, including Ammonius and Moseus, Nereus and Achilleus, Emeterius and Chelidonius, Juventinus and Maximinus; the list goes on.[2]

2. If you read ahead, you might even speculate that I would add to this list the spiritual union of T. Bennett and J. LaPointe, as well as the Hofer and Perkins brothers.

> "For most of the early church, there was no 'Don't ask, don't tell' policy in place when it came to being public about their faith. Rome did not make concessions—it made martyrs."

For most of the early church, there was no "Don't ask, don't tell" policy in place when it came to being public about their faith. Rome did not make concessions—it made martyrs. Soldier saints of this era had particular strength and courage, not only keeping their secret hidden while encouraging others facing death, but living in constant fear of being exposed and having their reputations and their lives taken violently from them.

★ ★ ★

God in three, we give thanks for your glorious martyrs, Sergius and Bacchus; their love for and dedication to each other is an inspiration and joy. These servants of the Lord, whose trust in the one true God, and Holy Trinity, was so great, that neither public humiliation, nor torture, nor threat of death swayed their devotion to Jesus, the Son of the Father. We pray for those in the military and armed forces throughout the world that they may always see God as their authority and obey his orders first. Amen.[3] ☧

3. Adapted from http://www.catholicdoors.com/prayers/novenas/p00086.htm, retrieved May 21, 2013.

Pachomius was the earliest saint with military history who was not martyred.[1] At a young age, he was conscripted into the Roman army from North Africa. He underwent all the training that soldiers received, including how to convert villages throughout the empire into fortified enclaves from which to coordinate military affairs. Forts were all over the Roman provinces, and many were built upon villages that had been abandoned or were taken by force into Roman control.[2]

For reasons little known, Pachomius refused to serve in some capacity and was therefore imprisoned before he ever saw combat or military service. In jail, Christian visitors would bring prisoners food, water, and general hospitality. Pachomius took a liking to their illegal religion. Before long, he was converted, baptized, and released from jail and from his military service obligation, but he never forgot his training.

He had a great admiration for the desert fathers, especially Saint Anthony, who was famous for his isolation and ascetic rigor. Christian

---

1. *The Life of Saint Pachomius, Abbot of Tabennisi, by an Unknown Greek Author* can be found online at http://www.vitae-patrum.org.uk/page11.html.
2. I owe much of this information to Dan Cantey's article in Volume 32, Number 2 of the *Journal of the Society for Christian Ethics*, "Can the Christian Serve in the Military? A Veteran Reflects on the Commensurability of the Christian Life and the Military Ethic," which he presented at a conference in Washington, D.C., in January 2012. Dan is a veteran and a wonderful scholar and teaches at Bethel University in Tennessee.

monks were largely *eremitic*,[3] leaving their urban lives behind in protest of both the state and the church, living alone in caves in the wilderness. But Pachomius was not called to be a solitary figure. After studying for seven years with an elder monk, he heard a voice telling him to "build a dwelling where many eager to embrace the monastic life" would come to him. So he put his old military training to good use. He gained a small following while he went about converting abandoned villages into small monastic communities. In fact, he became the father of communal monasticism, known as *cenobitic* monasticism. All the hermits and monks before him lived alone, but Pachomius lived in the company of other holy people like him.

"Pachomius's formation first as a soldier and later as a Christian was essential to his understanding of the communality of our faith."

Military training is timeless in its emphasis on camaraderie, training men and women to recognize their dependence upon others and others' dependence upon them. The phalanx of ancient Greece, which heavily shaped later Roman military strategy, was composed of soldiers tightly massed together for protection during an advance. The soldier on your left and right depended on you and you on them. Lone, isolated fighters were easily identified, engaged, and defeated. Similarly, the Christian faith has emphasized that it is "where two or three gather"[4] that Christ lives. Believers worship and break bread together, wash the feet of and pray with hands upon one another. Pachomius's formation first as a soldier and later as a Christian was essential to his understanding of the communality of our faith.

Not only was Pachomius the first soldier saint not martyred, he was also the first cenobitic monk, the founder of what is now a much more

3. *Eremetic* is a root of the word *hermit*, as well as implying a relationship to the desert. Prior to Pachomius, all monks lived alone in the desert like Anthony before them.
4. Matthew 18:20.

popular form of monastic life. Just like some branches of the military have core values expected of each soldier, sailor, marine, or airman,[5] Pachomius wrote a rule of life that would later be imitated by more famous monks, particularly Saint Benedict. By the time he died, there were nine male communities for Pachomius's order and two for women. Pachomius was so popular his bishop, Athanasius of Alexandria, tried to lay hands on him and coerce him into the priesthood, but Pachomius would have none of it and fled. None of the three thousand Pachomian monks in history were ever ordained; all have been lay people who answered the call to a radical community whose origins can be traced to the same communal standards with which soldiers are so familiar.

★ ★ ★

God, who is mysteriously one and yet three, your servant Pachomius has blessed the lives of monastics old and new by his life in community, which was marked by ascetic rigor, simple piety, and emphasis on the laity. You alone, God, create from nothing, and we give thanks for Pachomius mining the depths of his military training and finding within it the virtue of a committed life together, building upon his martial experience in obedience to your Word, our Lord. Give us the virtues necessary to live lives similarly obedient, through Christ Jesus. Amen. ☧

5. The United States "Army Values," for example, roughly spell out the acronym "leadership": loyalty, duty, respect, selfless service, honor, integrity, and personal courage.

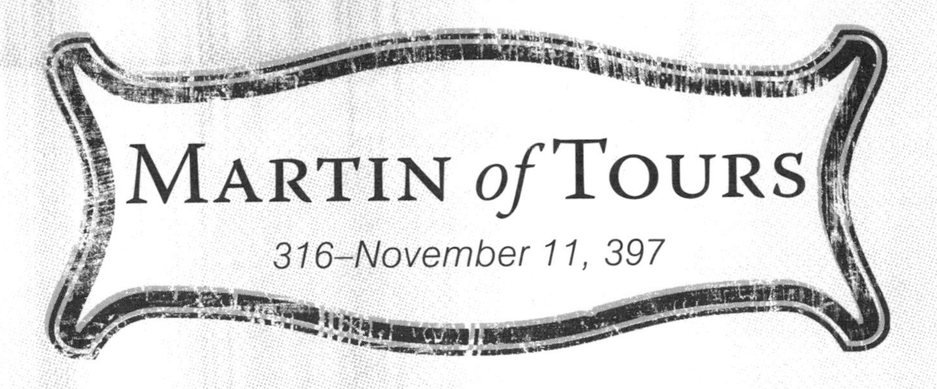

Martin of Tours

316–November 11, 397

Before there was Veterans Day (Remembrance Day in Canada), there was Armistice Day. Before Armistice Day, there was Martinmas—the feast for Martin of Tours, the patron saint of soldiers and chaplains. Martin lived during the fourth century in and around Rome, a centurion named in honor of Mars, the Roman god of war. His own father was from modern-day Hungary and became a prestigious military officer who intended to groom his young son to become a great soldier himself (an enforceable practice in the Roman Empire). Sometimes, however, it can be a good thing when we don't meet our parents' expectations.

"Many soldier converts, upon their baptism, renounced their service and were subsequently tried and often executed."

Martin had been religiously inclined since his childhood, indicating at an early age his interest in being baptized. This obviously conflicted with his eventual military occupational specialty, which was to be a part of the Praetorian Guard, the personal security detachment for Caesar Julian. Members of this elite unit were all bestowed with an elegant white lambskin cape, which signified their assignment to guard the emperor. One of the best-known tales about Martin concerns his splitting in half the cloak in order to clothe a freezing beggar. He is often depicted upon a great steed, another symbol of his special placement, bending down to hand half his cape to a half-naked beggar.

According to Martin's friend and biographer, Sulpitius Severus, the event took place just a few years into his service. That night he had a dream of Jesus, who said to the heavens, "Here is Martin, not even baptized, who has clothed me." Needless to say, Martin was baptized the very next morning.

Many soldier converts, upon their baptism, renounced their service and were subsequently tried and often executed.[1] Some have assumed that this was the case with Martin as well, but it is not so. Preparing for battle against the Franks nearly twenty years after Martin's baptism, Julian lined his men up to distribute generous gifts intended to secure their loyalty in combat. Martin knew he could not accept the combat pay, given his Christian convictions. As Julian approached him, he said, "I have been your soldier up to now. Let me now be God's. Let someone who is going to fight have your bonus. I am a soldier of Christ; I am not allowed to fight."

"I have been your soldier up to now. I am a soldier of Christ; I am not allowed to fight."

Julian flew into a rage, accusing the young soldier of cowardice. He had Martin locked up while he considered what to do with the seditious centurion. From his cell, Martin offered to be put on the front lines, without his weapons or armor. The emperor jumped at the chance to send the offending centurion to a certain death, and preparations were made. Miraculously, the Franks petitioned for peace and the battle was averted. What was the emperor to do? Martin was discharged the next day and immediately devoted himself to the religious life,

1. Nearly every soldier convert prior to Martin was martyred (Pachomius is a notable but rare exception), but in Martin's time it could go either way; the open persecution ended in 312 CE with Constantine I, but sporadic incidents continued to occur as Romans adjusted to the newly legalized religion. For example, Saints Juventinus and Maximinus served under Julian in the Praetorian Guard *with* Martin, but suffered martyrdom after being exposed as Christians as late as 363 CE. Victricius, on the other hand, fifteen years Martin's junior, was beaten severely but spared execution. In fact, Victricius went on to become Bishop of Rouen and involved himself with many of the same theological disputes in which Martin engaged.

becoming a monk for a time before he sought instruction from a wise theologian in Poitiers (in what is now France). He acquired the title "of Tours" when the people of that town dragged him into the city center and appointed him bishop by acclamation.[2]

In spite of all the expectations people held, his parents, the beggar, and his commander, Martin proved his duty was first to God. When he lay down his sword before God by being baptized, he knew he could not again pick it up for Caesar. He served his governing authority to the extent that his conscience allowed and volunteered his life to be used by God. After his death, the cape he split in half became a cherished relic in France, and the monks responsible for guarding it became the earliest "chaplains."

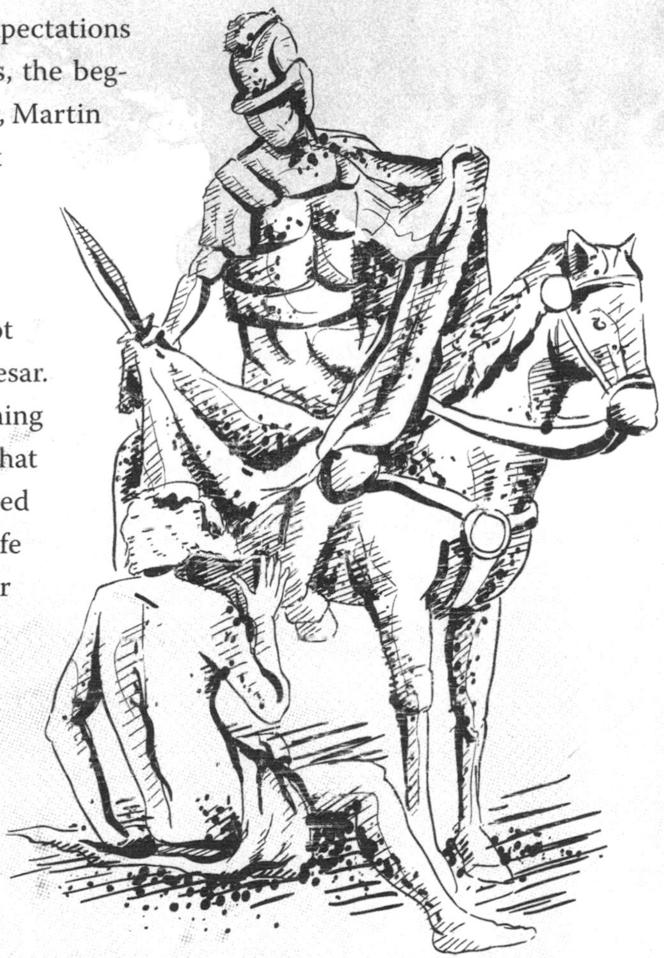

2. Ironically, the patron saint of soldiers, a conscientious objector, was acclaimed bishop on July 4, 370 CE—1,400 years before the birth of the United States of America as a nation. For men who felt that a standing army was "the bane of freedom," this anecdote might have made them chuckle in approval. The best biography of Martin was written by the French historian Regine Pernoud, which you can find in English as *Martin of Tours: Soldier, Bishop, Saint* (San Francisco, CA: Ignatius Press, 2006), based on the fourth-century document by Martin's close friend Sulpitius Severus, titled simply *The Life of Saint Martin*, which can be found online at http://www.newadvent.org/fathers/3501.htm.

★ ★ ★

God, grant us the courage to follow the example of Martin, who refused to carry both the sword and cross at once, who knew he was protected by the sign of the cross, not by helmet and shield. Your will be done. Though we have fought the good fight long enough, give us the strength, if you bid us continue in your service, to never beg to be excused from failing strength. While you alone command, we will serve beneath your banner, through Christ our Lord. Amen.[3]

I come from the military and offer to you [perspective] from someone on the outsid who was once on the inside. I was a Navy Corpsman (equivalent to an Army battlefield medic) stationed with Marine Corps infantry unit 3/1.

...I was a "connected member" of a Baptist church ...and yet I followed the military to war with Iraq. I was ready to kill to defend my own life and life of my patients in combat.

By the grace of God I was never offered a chance to pull the trigger of my weapon, and so never did

3. Adapted from "Letters of Sulpitius Severus (Undoubted)," in *A Select Library of Nicene and Post-Nicene Fathers of the Christian Church*, Second Series, Volume XI, ed. Philip Schaff and Henry Wace (Grand Rapids, MI: Eerdmans, 1997), 22–23. I shared this prayer at the commissioning of an icon of Martin that our student group commissioned Father Bill McNichols to create for the After the Yellow Ribbon conference, held November 11–12, 2011. You can download most of the seminars from the conference at http://www.sites.duke.edu/aftertheyellowribbon/schedule. You can view the prayer card produced for the icon online at http://loganmehllaituri.com/2012/02/08/martin-soldier-of-christ-icon-commentary.

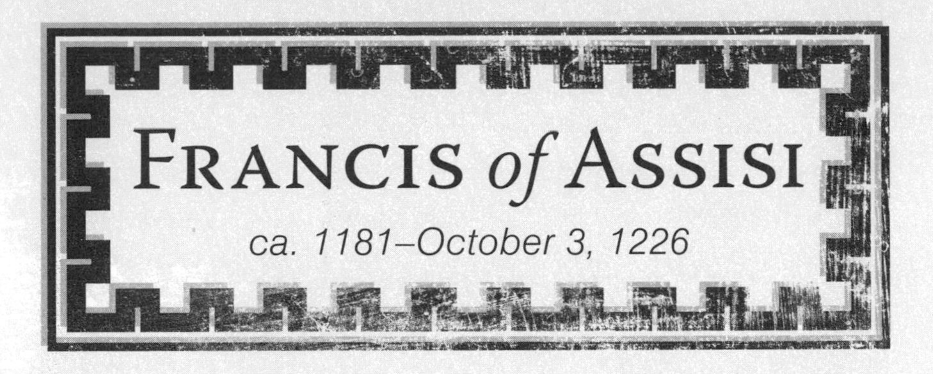

Francis is well known for his work reforming the Roman Catholic Church after a vision he had at a church in San Damiano, Italy. Jesus appeared to him, saying, "Francis, repair my church." He became an advocate for the poor, preached to the animals, and even tried to convert an Egyptian sultan. He founded a religious order once his mendicant followers became too numerous, pleading his cause for the "Order of Friars Minor" before the Vatican, and apparently shaming church hierarchy by his audacious acts of charity toward the poor. So many voluntarily destitute friars only highlighted the opulence of the Roman Catholic Church; the Vatican did not need this attention.

Today, Francis is widely known as the founder of the Franciscans, friars and priests committed to living the Rule of Saint Francis, including a vow of poverty. He is one of the most famous saints, in part because his order is so large. Francis is also popular among military chaplains, and it is not uncommon to see a prayer attributed to him adorning their offices. The famous Prayer of Saint Francis begins with "Lord, make me an instrument of your peace."[1] He even apparently has his own military weapons arsenal installation in St. Augustine, Florida!

It should not surprise us that Francis is associated with the military. After all, he was a soldier, having participated in a military campaign against the Italian town of Perugia in 1201 CE.[2] The episode ended

1. See page 188 for more on this peculiar prayer and its military-related background.
2. According to Jeff Matsler, a military chaplain and a classmate of mine, the campaign was actually a small Crusade declared by the pope after the merchants of Assisi rebeled by refusing to pay certain taxes. Their archenemy, a city across the river called Perugia, was only too happy to indulge. Jeff's presentation "Post Traumatic Saint: Understanding Healing and

tragically, as Francis was taken as a prisoner of war, one of only nine survivors from Assisi. He was released by ransom, but he would never be the same. He was known to have trouble sleeping because of nightmares, people witnessed him talking to himself or to animals, and he had anxiety issues. He was not unlike many war-weary veterans in our own day.

"Francis had a strange vision that convinced him to literally turn his back on the battlefield. Leaving the promise of glory behind him, he pursued the Prince of Peace and settled for rags over riches."

Then again in 1204, he set his feet upon the road to war, this time toward the Fourth Crusade. He hoped to return a prince, with all the glory and prestige afforded knights who returned safely from the Crusades. He returned with a different kind of crown entirely. Just a few days out from Assisi, Francis had a strange vision that convinced him to literally turn his back on the battlefield. Leaving the promise of glory behind him, he pursued the Prince of Peace and settled for rags over riches.

But he never turned his back on his fellow soldiers. In fact, eight of the first ten men who followed him in his life of poverty were veterans of the same campaigns in which he fought.[3]

Resiliency Through the Life of Saint Francis of Assisi," was released December 6, 2012, on iTunesU: https://itunes.apple.com/us/itunes-u/milites-christi/id477245098.

3. This figure, eight of the first ten of his followers, was cited by Chaplain Matsler in his presentation, which none of the three history professors in attendance disputed.

He is known for his work with animals, often retreating to the wilderness to preach to the flora and fauna. Every October, many churches bless their animals, as Francis was thought to have blessed the beasts of the field. But there is another way to see this. Veterans' rehabilitation groups now offer low-cost "emotional support animals" to help traumatized veterans recovering from the hidden wounds of war. This begs the question of Francis: was he blessing the animals, or were they blessing him?

"Was he blessing the animals, or were they blessing him?"

Francis's ties to war were great, and are often overlooked. But he was a soldier through and through. Like military leaders in today's armed forces, he never asked his followers to do anything he himself had not already done—whether fasting or begging for alms. His loyalty to the church to which he belonged was learned in the fiery fields of battle with which he was familiar. One of the most recognized religious figures in history was not just a pious man; he was a soldier saint, a true reflection of God in our broken world.

★ ★ ★

God of the earth and everything on it, you gave us your servant Francis, who brought your glory to all the world and all who live in it. May we, by his example, come to a greater thankfulness for your creation, the beauty of the land, and our fellow creatures that walk, swim, and fly therein. Keep our hand from war as you did with brave Francis. Convict our hearts to love the flora and fauna as readily as we do our fellow human beings. Strengthen our efforts at peace, both before violence breaks out and after it subsides. Help us to care equally for those we send and those we receive, that we may honor the created dignity of their lives as we honor the life of this, your most holy servant, with the help of your Son, Jesus Christ. Amen.

Joan of Arc was born into simplicity and poverty. For her entire life, she could neither read nor write. She was very young when she began hearing and seeing angels, including Michael the archangel, telling her that God would use her to restore her own King Charles VII to the French throne, despite her motherland being oppressively ruled by the English. With no combat experience, she went to her deposed king and prophesied that she would free the besieged city of Orleans, which would lead to Charles's coronation as king. Intrigued but cautious, Charles had her examined thoroughly by priests and theologians to determine her theological reliability and her sincerity, much like conscientious objectors in today's military are examined.

After intense scrutiny, she passed with flying colors. Only seventeen years old at the time, she was found to be exceedingly humble, honest, and devoted to the simple life of a holy person. Though others would contrive majestic and prosaic names for her, she refused to call herself anything but "Joan the Maid." With her assistance, Orleans

was indeed recaptured from its siege by the English, and Charles was crowned soon thereafter. In all, she spent about one year in the companies of France and her armies.

After her participation in the recapture of Orleans, however, Joan grew listless and perhaps a bit overconfident. She wrote letters to heretics making threats of "taking away either [their] heresy or [their] lives."[1] She engaged in earthly battles left unmentioned by her celestial friends Michael and Saints Margaret and Catherine. At the battle that would prove to be her last, she took the place of honor in the struggling rear guard so that she would be the last standing on the field of battle. Captured by Burgundians, she was quickly sold to her enemies for ransom; her own poor family could not purchase her and her king had had a cowardly change of heart. Joan would remain a prisoner of war for about a year, the same time she spent in the French army.

The English, whom she had shamed terribly by defeating them at Orleans, were bound and determined to convict Joan of heterodoxy, even though she had passed the rigorous examination by French ecclesiastical authorities. The English-aligned bishop Pierre Cauchon (whose name in French means "swine") was assigned to oversee the trial. When she appealed to the shared authority of the pope, Cauchon refused to allow messengers to be sent or even to admit non-English religious authorities to the court. The technical charge dealt with a biblical clothing law, which Joan violated by having dressed as a man from the time she joined the French army in order to avoid being molested or raped while on campaign. Several theologians testified in her defense that her dress actually maintained her chastity, but it was a kangaroo court that finally concluded with the illiterate defendant signing an admission to heresy—a capital offense.

Just two years after coming onto the European scene in a major way, Joan was killed. Her final word, according to numerous eyewitnesses,

1. *Joan of Arc; Her Story*, by Regine Pernoud (Hampshire, England: Palgrave Macmillan, 1999), 258.

was "Jesus." She was exonerated in 1456 and called a martyr, while Cauchon was ironically condemned as a heretic for pursuing a political vendetta and being responsible for the death of an innocent young woman.

★ ★ ★

Even though Joan is seen as a military hero and saint, she also points to nonviolence and peace. There is growing evidence to suggest that Joan never actually wielded the sword. In fact, based on testimony from the original trial, it is clear that Joan "preferred the standard to the sword." In other words, she was a guidon bearer who happened to be a courageous and skilled martial tactician with a strong sense of national identity, pride, and piety. At the

But I'm miserable living this life I am, when i know another one is possible. An amazing, God-pleasing life at that I just don't know what to do. I am so torn I feel like it would be so [much] easier being a man (probably not though, huh??) but nevertheless, I do. ... I want to follow jesus, but I feel like i'm at such a crossroads.

least, humble Joan the Maid reminds us that it is not solely for their national identity or pride that saints are remembered but for their extreme piety, no matter the specific mission to which they are called. Politics are also subordinate to justice and mercy; God uses the meek to overthrow the strong, not the other way around.

★ ★ ★

God of justice and peace, we give thanks for the blessed martyr Joan, with whom we may receive the eyes to see visions and the ears to hear the voices of the saints before us. Grant us the grace to honor our rulers, yet temper the grace with the wisdom to rebuke them when we must. Keep us from the dangers of restlessness, of overstepping our bounds, and of missing the mustard seed of grace. When we fail, keep us from pride and restore to us a contrite heart as you did for the courageous Joan; may her witness remind us that though our enemies may discredit us, we take heart in knowing that our vindication is through Christ Jesus, our Lord. Amen. ☧

"Grant us the grace to honor our rulers, yet temper the grace with the wisdom to rebuke them when we must."

JOHN *of* GOD

1495–March 8, 1550

John was a Portuguese soldier who served Charles V of Spain in arms against the French and later in Austria against the Turks under the Count of Oropesa, Fernando Alvarez. In all, he spent about eighteen years in martial service, during which, by all accounts, he left the faith of his youth behind, taking up gambling and drinking in its stead. By the time he tired of his martial exploits, he had come near to absolute poverty and is known to some as a "waif"—abandoned, alone, and without a home. John's fate was not unlike many soldiers of our day who are disproportionately homeless, substance addicted, and suffering from broken homes, broken relationships, and broken hearts.

Filled with the desire to mend his ways, John went about employing himself in all manner of charitable works. In Grenada, Spain, he served a family exiled near Gibraltar. At a hospital in Grenada, he rescued many patients caught in a massive fire, without him being burned. Well acquainted with bravery from his time on the battlefield, John felt at home serving those in need and in danger, even while he himself might be put in need and find himself in harm's way.

Finding only sporadic outlets for his penitential stress, he continued to feel tormented by guilt and constantly sought absolution. That

very few people . . . know what to do with veterans. . . . We stay clear of places like the VA because they always try to convince us we're sick. [I] flee from people who want to [c]all me a victim, and cling to people who lift up

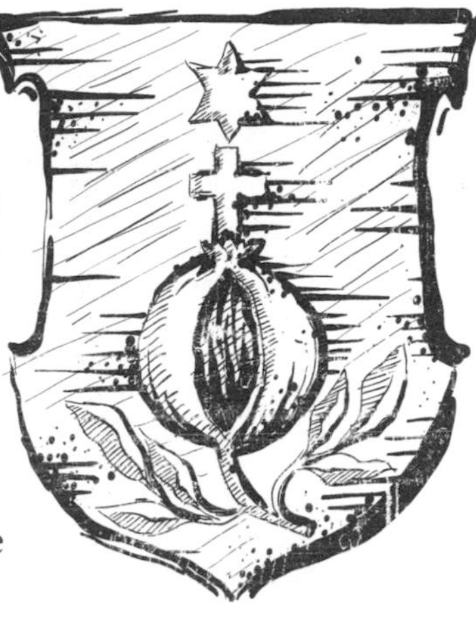

is, until the feast day of another soldier saint, Sebastian, on January 20, 1538. Hearing a sermon from John of Avila (the native town of Sebastian), he began to wail uncontrollably before throwing himself onto the street, beating his breast, tearing his hair, and crying to God for mercy. So boisterous was his penance that he was committed to an insane asylum.

In the asylum, he witnessed the utterly depraved treatment of people who were mentally ill and disabled. By the time he would otherwise have been released, he had begun to serve his fellow inmates. John became convinced that his life was to be lived in service to the sick and poor, just as he had once been. He prayed, "May Jesus Christ give me the grace to run a hospital where the abandoned poor and those who suffer mental illness may have refuge, so that I may be able to serve them as I wish."

This proved to be the foundation for an order he went on to found in 1572, known as the Brothers Hospitallers. To this day the Hospitallers are entrusted with the medical and dental care of the pope himself.[1] In Italian, they are known as the *Fatebenefratelli*, the "Do Good Brothers," for their founding and continued operation of the busiest pharmacy in the world, located on the grounds of Vatican City

1. His order (http://www.hospitallers.org) must not be confused with the Knights Hospitaller, who (beside the Knights Templar) were a major military order that undertook the Crusades. In fact, Charles V, under whom John served, was partially responsible for reviving the militaristic order. Not to be confused with Crusaders, the Order of Knights of Saint John of God, formed only in 2005, protect the saint's relics in Grenada. They carry no weapons and their motto is simply "God is love."

in Rome. John's final act of heroism was a failed attempt to save a young man from drowning, which led to an undisclosed and fatal illness (perhaps pneumonia). He died on his fifty-fifth birthday in 1550.

"He was able to turn the passion and dedication he learned while in the military into protecting and caring for those who were not seen as mentally stable."

Like many soldiers today, John was thought to be mad, perhaps as a result of his time on the battlefield.[2] The connection between mental health in the hospitals of Grenada in the sixteenth century and the veterans' hospitals today is not hard to make. John knew what it was to be abandoned, poor, and alone. His prayer to God was almost certainly a petition for himself as well as for other "abandoned poor" and homeless people such as veterans who suffer posttraumatic stress disorder and moral injuries. He was able to turn the passion and dedication he learned while in the military into protecting and caring for those who, like himself, were not seen as mentally stable.

★ ★ ★

God of order and love, Prince of Peace and Justice, bear me against your breast in my darkest moments, shield me from invasive thoughts and the harrowing of a conscience crystallized too late. Take a towel to dry my night sweats, a damp cloth to moisten my dried lips. Guard my mind from painful memories and deliver my dreams from the evil I've seen and done and failed to prevent. Protect me from my own past, dear Lord, and comfort me in my grief. Overcome my fear with your perfect love. Grant me your peace in wakefulness and sleep, through the mercy of your Son, our Savior, Jesus Christ. Amen.

2. Learn more about posttraumatic stress at http://www.ptsd.va.gov. Also see *Beyond the Yellow Ribbon: Ministering to Returning Combat Veterans*, by D. A. Thompson and D. Wetterstrom (Nashville, TN: Abingdon Press; 2009), and MennoMedia's pamphlet *Posttraumatic Stress Disorder* (Harrisonburg, VA: 2012).

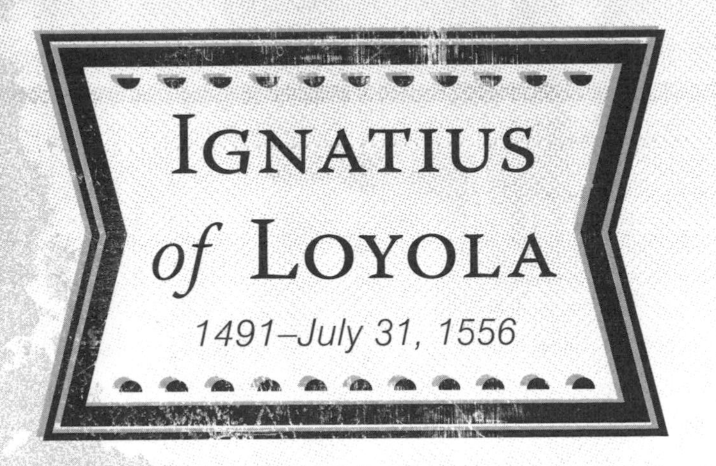

Ignatius was born in Spain to a noble family, one year before Christopher Columbus would sail for America from Spain. Inigo, as he was called at birth, would grow to become a knight and fight in many battles for other Spanish nobility, proudly walking through town between campaigns wearing his vest of chain mail and his magnificent armaments. Never far from the faith, Ignatius claimed he was a cleric while he was in court defending himself after a violent feud with another noble family.

During a battle against the French, his legs were seriously injured, leaving him at the mercy of his opponents. Recognizing his honorable conduct in the fight, the French did not ask for ransom as they did others, instead carrying him gently back to a castle where he could be given proper medical attention. Ignatius wrestled with vanity, however, so when surgery left him with a bony lump on his knee, he endured great pain to have the protruding bone chiseled down. The procedure left him with a limp not unlike that of Jacob, who wrestled with God.[1]

While recuperating, all he had to read was a copy of the Gospels and a book on the lives of Christian saints. Reading about the Christian life had a profound effect on him; though his physical wounds would heal, the spiritual tumult caused by the lives of which he read would infect him for life.

1. Genesis 32:22-32.

For some time the young injured knight had wrestled with his call toward faith in God and service to his neighbors. To an extent he was still a young man devoted to martial and flirtatious exploits. But during his period of convalescence, he weighed a future of womanizing and fighting against a future of piety. When he thought of the life of a playboy, he was filled with excitement and anticipation, but it would fade quickly as he moved on to other thoughts. But when he thought of the life of a disciple, taking the good news to the corners of the earth, his heart flamed long after his lustful and militaristic thoughts fizzled. Heroism never ceased to be an interest for Ignatius; it just took a different form. His new heroes were priests and monks instead of princes and knights.

Traveling by mule after this initial evangelical experience, he encountered another rider, who challenged him on the doctrine concerning the virginity of Mary. Falling slightly behind the man but still aflame with zeal, he longed to slay the man, but Ignatius stayed his hand so

that he could obtain a sign from God. Dropping his reins at a fork in the road, he reasoned that if the unguided mule followed the traveler, Ignatius would kill the man. If the mule took its own path, the knight would show mercy. The ass, like Balaam's before him, guided the soon-to-be-saint in godly charity.[2]

In 1522 he visited a Benedictine monastery where he wrestled one last time between the life of a knight and the life of a religious man. Before a statue of Mary, Ignatius laid down his sword and shield, never to pick them back up. He went on to form the Company of Jesus, fashioned after a military company; in fact the papal statement granting them legitimacy is translated from Latin as "the governance of the militant" ("the militant," presumably, meaning Ignatius and his companions).[3] To this day, Jesuits are known as God's Marines, for they take vows of poverty, chastity, and obedience, especially to the pope. Just as Marines defend the country, Jesuits "strive especially for . . . the defense of the faith." The head of the order is even known as the superior *general*, suggesting a military rank. Ignatius was elected, against his will like Martin before him, to serve in the high rank as the order's first superior general.

Like Francis, Ignatius of Loyola was another founding father of an organization within the church. He was a thinking man; appropriately, many Jesuit institutions are educational. Georgetown University and Boston College, and publications like *America Magazine* and Ignatius Press, grow out of the work of the Jesuits. Ignatius, reflecting the discipline of his military background, developed spiritual exercises to help form Christians in the faith. Among these was the Daily Examen of Conscience:[4]

---

2. Numbers 22:21-32.

3. A "papal bull" is a statement issued by the pope that is sealed with a stamp, which in Latin is a *bulla*. The Latin title of the bull in question was *regimini militantis ecclesiae*, the "Government of the Church Militant."

4. Loyola Press, the Ignatian publishing house, has a great website on how to familiarize yourself with Ignatian spirituality: http://www.ignatianspirituality.com/ignatian-prayer/the-examen.

1. Become aware of God's presence.
2. Review the day with gratitude.
3. Pay attention to your emotions.
4. Choose one feature of the day and pray from it.
5. Look toward tomorrow.

★ ★ ★

Christian soldiers are called to conduct an examen of their own consciences daily. Our service is to God first, and to country only secondarily. We must constantly search our consciences for those moments and circumstances that violate our conscience, and "obey God rather than [the officers appointed above us]" as needed.[5] Like Ignatius, we may need to lay our weapons down before the altar in answer to our call to discipleship.

Lord of all nations, we give thanks for the life of your servant Ignatius, who by the mercy of your Son overcame his tempestuous life and adopted simplicity and love, guided by your Spirit to study, contemplation, and prayer. We ask for your strength in daily discerning your will for our lives, in examining our consciences in all we do, especially when violence calls our name. May we live in accordance with the witness of this soldier saint, who dedicated his life to structure and discipline, whose love gave those in his company shape and direction. Through Jesus Christ, commander of heaven and earth. Amen.

"Like Ignatius, we may need to lay our weapons down before the altar in answer to our call to discipleship."

5. Adapted from Acts 5:29, New Revised Standard Version.

Camillus of Lellis

1550–July 16, 1614

The image of a red cross has become a global symbol of medical assistance in conflict-ridden areas. Internationally, the modern Red Cross organizes disaster relief and protects victims of armed conflict, including combatants, refugees, and prisoners of war. The group has won three Nobel Peace Prizes for acting as a neutral mediator between states in conflict, among other incredible feats. Many think that prior to the Red Cross's founding in the eighteenth century, no organized, well-established army nursing systems for casualties existed, nor any safe and protected institutions to accommodate and treat those wounded on the battlefield. But Saint Camillus's story proves otherwise.

Like many volunteers in today's military forces, Camillus enlisted at only seventeen years of age, in 1567, in the same Venetian legion his father had served. Sometime during his many years in the military, he sustained a leg wound that failed to properly heal. Camillus knew well the suffering of those in war and elsewhere. He also shared with many soldiers and veterans a penchant for gambling and risk-taking that marks the martial fraternity even today.

In the midst of his military career, he encountered several monastic orders in which he developed an interest, but which refused to admit him, possibly on account of his active duty service in the Venetian army. Perhaps feeling religiously slighted, he returned to battle, this time against the Turks. In 1574, his regiment was disbanded and he went to work for a group of Capuchin friars, an offshoot of the Franciscan order. These men had such an effect on him that he was fully converted within a year. His attempts to join the order were denied repeatedly on account of his leg wound, but he was permitted to be a lay brother for a time.

He was quite familiar with hospitals as a frequent patient for either his incurable leg or injuries he sustained as a result of drinking or gambling during his military service. Determined to become a priest, he moved to Rome and began rising in the ranks of the Hospital for Incurables there, first as a nurse and eventually assuming the role of director. His resumé reflected his improving demeanor, and many in Rome saw his success not just in the hospital but also in the city; in the face of the bubonic plague he was known as the Saint of Rome. On Pentecost in 1584, he was finally ordained and briefly left the hospital for the seminary. He studied at the newly established Jesuit college in Rome,[1] where he would establish a new religious order, the Clerks Regular, Ministers to the Infirm (abbreviated M.I.). In 1591, Pope Gregory XV elevated Camillus and his followers—the Camillians—to a full order, recognizing the former Venetian soldier's pioneering care not just in hospitals, but also at the homes of the sick and, soon, right in the midst of battle he knew so well as a youth. It was this effort that led to the establishment of a ministry that cared for wounded soldiers on the battlefield—the first field medical unit.

The wounded piled up so quickly in some units that their own comrades buried some alive in their haste. Camillus ordered his men to wait no less than fifteen minutes after the last sign of life to protect the unconscious wounded soldiers from this awful fate. To clearly mark themselves as neutral ministers to the sick on both sides of the fight, Camillus needed a symbol that combatants could identify from

1. The very first university established by the Jesuits, in 1551, it is today known as the Pontifical Gregorian University.

afar. The cross was an obvious choice, but not the usual earthen tone of brown or black. He chose instead to use a bright red to stand out on the Camillians' dark habits (the simple garments of monks and itinerant priests).

During the Battle of Canizza in 1601, the tent out of which the brothers operated caught fire and everything inside was destroyed, except for a swatch of dark clothing surrounding the red cross emblematic of Camillus's order. The Camillians took this as a divine sign of approval for the work they did on the battlefield. The red cross thus came into being in the seventeenth century, long before the Red Cross was formed as an international organization. Long before there were organization mission statements, Camillians vowed "to serve the sick, even with danger to one's own life."[2]

"The hospital was 'a house of God, a garden where the voices of the sick were music from heaven.'"

Caring for the sick is always a trying endeavor. One sees ghastly wounds and unquenchable human distress and despair in war. Medics on battlefields see all kinds of obscenities that war produces, and depression is a real threat. But Jesus told Camillus, "Fear not, for this is not your work, but mine." Just as he found courage on the battlefield, Camillus overcame fear with faith, hope, and love. He taught the brothers of his order that the hospital was "a house of God, a garden where the voices of the sick were music from heaven."[3] He himself died in 1614 and we celebrate his life on the day of his death, on July 14th.

★ ★ ★

2. Roman Catholic religious orders all make at least three vows, of poverty, chastity, and obedience. This fourth vow taken by Camillians reflects the centrality of bodily sacrifice for the order established by Camillus, which is somewhat similar to the readiness of military personnel to risk their lives for the sake of others. Learn more at http://www.camillians.org.
3. http://www.camillians.org/History.php, retrieved May 21, 2013.

Lord God almighty, who descended into hell in order to liberate the oppressed, we thank you for the witness of your servant Camillus, who, after having been set free by the blessing of the cross, followed your Son's example by returning to the hell of war, bearing the very sign of his redemption to the wounded and weary in need. May his courage and humility continue to bless our lives and make possible our own humble confidence in the face of overwhelming danger and temptation, through Jesus Christ, our heavenly commander. Amen. ☧

John Vianney

1786–August 4, 1859

John Vianney became interested in the priesthood from an early age while working on his family's farm in France. Early in his life, the French countryside was ablaze in the fire of revolution and revolt. Many souls turned from God, and John later reflected that religious ignorance and intolerance was the bitter fruit of the labor for secular political change. Priests, during this time, were forced to perform services in secret, and John gained a great respect for the work of pastors who defied social circumstances in order to be true to their vocation.

In 1809, at seventeen years of age, John was drafted into Napoleon's armies during the emperor's Peninsular War against Spain. John should have been exempted as a seminary student, but times were tough and recruitment was low.[1] The law is sometimes flexible in times of war, it would seem. Spain was, to the French emperor, a clear and present danger to his continued expansion. So off John went for training, but he fell seriously ill along the way.

---

1. The military exemption for seminarians and priests is ages old. During Vietnam, they fell under the same Selective Service category as those mentally and physically incapable of military service.

After he recovered, he found the conscripts had left without him, so he was sent elsewhere for another round of conscription, which he did not refuse. At a church in Roanne, he prayed fervently, for what nobody knows, during which he again fell behind his cohort. He enlisted the help of a guide to take him to where he would be trained to serve Napoleon, but instead, he was taken to a town filled with deserters.

There, he took a false name and carried out a different kind of training that evoked in him memories of the secret services that prepared him for baptism and confirmation; he opened a school for children under his assumed identity. He and the other deserters carried on in secret under fake names, often hiding in hay bales or in basements until March of 1810, when an imperial decree granted amnesty to all deserters.

John wanted to become a parish priest in Ars, France, but had trouble passing his Latin exams. The bishop was loathe to ordain him, but relented in 1815. Three years later, John inherited the church in Ars upon the death of his mentor, who had preached there. He quickly became widely known for being able to cure the souls of people, to look deeply into their sins and aid them in profound confessions. Pilgrims began to flock there to witness John's amazing talent for pastoring troubled souls toward reconciliation with God. He was known to have supernatural skill in seeing sins and transgressions without having to be told of them in the confessional booth.

John Vianney died August 4, 1859, with thousands in attendance at his funeral. He is the patron of priests and pastors and Pope Benedict XVI, himself a military deserter, evoked his memory during a "Year for Priests" during the 2009–10 liturgical calendar. His memory reminds us that evading the powers that be is not in itself cowardly or impious. In his own self-imposed exile, we can more fully understand American draft dodgers and deserters living in Canada and elsewhere, who also cannot bring themselves to submit to governing authorities out of sync with their moral consciences. Though it may be difficult for many patriotic citizens to treat deserters with love, the patron of priests guides in doing just that. John Vianney's prayer, printed below, reminds us of the fourth chapter of the New Testament's epistle of John, insisting boldly that "God is love."

★ ★ ★

I love you, O my God, and my only desire is to love you until the last breath of my life. I love you, O my infinitely lovable God, and I would rather die loving you than live without loving you. I love you, Lord, and the only grace I ask is to love you eternally. My God, if my tongue cannot say in every moment that I love you, I want my heart to repeat it to you as often as I draw breath. Amen.[2]

2. Adapted from http://www.stjohnvianneykamloops.ca/saint-john-vianney, retrieved May 22, 2013.

Franz Jägerstätter*

1907–August 9, 1943

Some traditions continue to carry on the practice of venerating holy men and women who exemplify holiness and profoundly faithful lives to be emulated. Saints continue to be found, even today—even in the midst of great evil that surrounds them.

One such recent saint is Franz Jägerstätter of Austria, born in 1907 to a couple too poor to be married. After his father died in World War I, a humble farmer adopted Franz and insisted he learn to read so that he could educate himself. He reveled in his youthfulness, becoming known as an unruly young man. However, he soon grew out of his rebellion and married in 1936, not long before the looming World War II would rear its ugly head.[1]

On his honeymoon in Rome, he visited the Vatican and happened upon a blessing from Pope Pius XI, which seemed to enliven his faith. He returned home and took up the task of Christian education after church on Sundays. He began giving alms to the poor, even though the

1. There were a number of conscientious objectors despite popular support of World War II. For a survey of some fine examples, see Mary R. Hopkins, *Men of Peace: World War II Conscientious Objectors* (Caye Caulker, Belize: Produccicones de la Hamaca, 2009) and Paul Wilhelm, *Civilian Public Servants: A Report on 210 World War II Conscientious Objectors* (Washington, DC: National Interreligious Service Board for Conscientious Objectors, 1990).

peasant farm life he led was not affluent. He is reported to have memorized huge swaths of the Bible and quoted Scripture like a scholar.

In 1938, he voted against the annexation of his home country by Germany (the only such vote cast in his entire village) and would get into heated conversations against Nazism in social gatherings. Some accounts suggest he served very briefly in the military, long enough for some training and long enough to find his conscience opposed to armed service, especially in an unjust cause. He offered to serve as a paramedic, as Mohandas Gandhi had in the Zulu and Boer wars of Britain, but his offer was denied.

"Neither prison nor chains nor sentence of death can rob a man of the faith and his free will. God gives so much strength that it is possible to bear any suffering."

As a farmer, he gained an exemption from soldiering on more than one occasion, but in February 1943, the final call came. He refused and was convicted of sedition by court martial. Many people, including his priest and the local bishop, visited him in prison to try to convince him that just a little compromise could spare him the guillotine, but to no avail. Franz was steadfast in his conviction. He would be beheaded, like Maximilian, Marcellus, and George before him.

As he was being led off to execution, he was offered a copy of the New Testament, which he kindly refused. "I am completely bound in inner union with the Lord," he said, "and any reading would only interrupt my communication with my God." Among his last words were "Neither prison nor chains nor sentence of death can rob a man of the faith and his free will. God gives so much strength that it is possible to bear any suffering." The priest who ministered to the imprisoned at Linz, where Franz was martyred, said bluntly "I can say with certainty that this simple man is the only saint I have met in my lifetime." His feast is on August 21, the day he was baptized.

> "The voice of the martyrs can help us discern where God begins and country ends, when our allegiance to the former precludes obedience to the latter."

For centuries after the persecution of Christians ended in ancient Rome, very few people were martyred for refusing military service. However, Franz reminds us that persecution for those who obey God rather than human leaders may come in many guises.[2] The accommodation between church and state in the modern era has brought a certain kind of peace, but any compromise is two-sided. How much do we compromise, and where is the line between just enough and too much? The clergy who consoled Franz had a point: he could escape

2. The word is rarely used because of its association with Nazi Germany, but *führer* translates simply to "leader, guide." It was used interchangeably for national leaders, like Hitler, and more local leaders and guides, like the priests and bishops who instructed stubborn Franz.

execution if he just did this one little thing. The voice of the martyrs can help us discern where God begins and country ends, when our allegiance to the former precludes obedience to the latter.

★ ★ ★

God over Israel and Germany, of Jew and Gentile alike, who kindled the flame of your forceful love in the heart of your holy martyr Franz Jägerstätter: grant to us a power of love like that which Franz displayed, that we may rejoice in his triumph and profit by his example. May we thereby commune with you without ceasing, praying with our very lives; it is you who call. Through Jesus Christ our Lord, who lives and reigns with you and the Holy Spirit, one God, for ever and ever. Amen. ☧

Part III

Pacifists *and* Pacific Patriots

One of the earliest ideas that I had for this book grew out of my own search for meaning and place within the church. I fell deeply in love with God, but had trouble finding God's church in the midst of two wars and a very polarized political atmosphere in the United States. Whether I liked it or not, a central aspect of my identity came from my active duty in the most powerful military force the world had yet seen.

The first books I read during this time were heavily theological, filled with lots of academic jargon that took me a good while to learn. Luckily I found some others that weren't so filled with technical language, books like the *American Patriot's Bible*[1] and *The American Patriot's Almanac: Daily Readings on America.*[2] I was about as patriotic as folks come, I thought; I had fought in war and was getting ready to do so a second time. But the way those latter books saw "patriotism" didn't match up with the pacifism I was reading about in theological books. I also came across the *Jesus Freaks* series, which included books on women,[3] martyrs,[4] and revolutionaries.[5] *Under God* was another book I found engaging, theologically nuanced, and compelling not just because of its overt patriotic focus, but also because it seemed to be willing to think through things other books on patriotism were not; like the idea that America had a checkered (not pristine) past.[6] I had a few objections, but in all, I genuinely appreciated the voices highlighted in these various books. The book you hold in your hand is meant to further diversify and expand upon stories and themes I first read about in those books.

1. By Richard Lee (Nashville, TN: Thomas Nelson, 2009), and online at http://www.americanpatriotsbible.com/.
2. By William Bennett and John Cribb (Nashville, TN: Thomas Nelson, 2008).
3. Rebecca St. James and Mary E. DeMuth, *Sister Freaks; Stories of Women Who Gave Up Everything for God* (New York: FaithWords, 2005).
4. DC Talk, *Martyrs Who Stood for Jesus, the Ultimate Jesus Freaks* (Minneapolis, MN: Bethany, 2005).
5. DC Talk, *Revolutionaries Who Changed Their World, Fearing God not Man* (Minneapolis, MN: Bethany, 2005).
6. Toby Mac and Michael Tait, *Under God* (Minneapolis, MN: Bethany, 2004).

The people I feature in this next segment are all heroic in their own ways. Not all fought in the military, but all were familiar with war and the sacrifice it demands. Many of them won the highest award their nation could bestow. In both the church and the state, we recognize those among us who are exemplars of the virtues that we think should shape our lives. For the church, that has historically been martyrdom, which was described since the first century as the seal and crown of our faith. For the United States military, the highest "crown" one can receive is the Congressional Medal of Honor, for acts of conspicuous valor in the face of danger. In the polarized political culture of the United States, I remember a radio show host or two getting up in arms about the "feminization" of the Medal of Honor, as many of the awards coming out of the "global war on terror" were given to those who saved, instead of took, lives.[7]

"One can serve God and country (in that order), since the interests of each will sometimes overlap. The difficult task is discerning when those interests are opposed."

Several Medal of Honor recipients throughout American history, however, did not even pick up a weapon. Chaplains, who have always been (and, I pray, always will be) unarmed in battle, have won at least eight of the prestigious awards. Others who are not chaplains also refused to carry a weapon, but did their duty honorably and are deserving of the highest accolades. Awards are not given to those who seek them, but those who seek only "the peace and prosperity of the city"[8] or nation to which they belong. One can serve God and country (in that order), since the interests of each will sometimes overlap. The difficult task is discerning when those interests are opposed and acting in conflict with each other.

7. "The Feminization of the Medal of Honor," by Bryan Fischer, can be read online at *Rightly Concerned*, http://www.afa.net/blogs/blogpost.aspx?id=2147500421.
8. Jeremiah 29:7.

Nations do not canonize their saints, though they do have exemplary heroes. These "saints" are the exemplars of a particular community, such as Medal of Honor winners, morally upright leaders, or social prophets. In this segment, as in part 2, I use asterisks in the profile titles to mark special recognition for sacrifice. A single asterisk indicates those who received the Medal of Honor or who died as martyrs for standing firm in their pacifist conviction. You might feel that placing traditional martyrs alongside contemporary national heroes is not quite right. Dwell in that place for a bit—consider how the two are similar and how they are different. Use correction fluid if you need to; it's okay. Unlike the canonized soldier saints from the previous section, I do not include prayers of those profiled here, since their memories are too fresh for adequate contemplation on their lives to emerge. In contrast to the formal beatification process for the saints of earlier church history, this selection is more personal.

Here, however, you will find a number of saints that finely balanced love of God over love of country, who gave to the powers that be what was theirs with kindness and respect. Not many of these would assent to the title *pacifist,* but we can think of them as those who have lived out alternative values from within the system. Most important to them was not the number of enemy they killed but a life lived well in light of a higher truth that took precedence over the values of their nation when those values conflicted with God's call.

"God bless your mother" was frequently repeated in one community I lived with not too long ago. For each of our birthdays, we would retell tales from our birth, in honor of the women who brought us into this earth. Similar stories often made it to the dinner table around Mother's Day, one of the holidays I used to think was an invention of Hallmark, Inc. In fact, Mother's Day has highly political origins, beginning with the famous American suffragette Julia Ward Howe.

Julia was a family woman. She and her husband Samuel Gridley Howe were abolitionists well before the outbreak of the Civil War. She and Samuel were also volunteers for the Sanitary Commission, battling the causes of disease that claimed more lives than outright combat would. Each was well known in their own right for similar commitments to justice, Samuel for his activism, Julia for her poetry and plays. In late 1861, President Lincoln himself invited them to Washington, D.C., for a military parade. There they overheard an army unit, calling military cadence about the origins of the Civil War, specifically about the body of John Brown.[1]

1. Cadence in the military is done while marching or running in formation. A call by the formation leader is followed by a response by those marching or walking. Many of them had to do with violence or sex, earning them the alternative title of "Jodies," after Jody, a male character featured in many popular cadences who steals your girlfriend while you are deployed away from home.

The song was a reference to the abolitionist who advocated violent action against slaveholders, culminating in the infamous Harpers Ferry incident in which he raided an armory to acquire weaponry to inspire and support a slave rebellion. Brown was wounded by Robert E. Lee during an intervention by United States Marines, and his subsequent trial in Virginia led to his hanging. Lyrics boldly compared him to one particular figure in the gospels:

John Brown was John the Baptist of the Christ we are to see,
Christ who of the bondmen shall the Liberator be.[2]

A clergyman attending the viewing with Julia, well aware of her writing talents, suggested she write a song to rally the soldiers, building morale for the war that lay ahead. That same night, she reported to friends, she awoke in the middle of the night, lyrics beginning to take shape within the preordained tune. She scribbled what she could in the dark of night as her children slept soundly in another room. The result was "The Battle Hymn of the Republic"; a song that would become and remain one of the most widely sung patriotic songs. Many Americans are probably still able to imagine the tune as they scan the opening line:

Mine eyes have seen the glory of the coming of the Lord

Not everyone remembers the rest of the song, whose lyrics align the Union's cause with Christ and compare the South with the serpent of Genesis:

I have read a fiery gospel writ in burnished rows of steel:
Let the Hero, born of woman, crush the serpent with his heel.

The popular hymn went on to become quite famous, and many lyrics have been superimposed upon hers, often with a similar convergence of faith and service. It has appeared in hymnals, regularly sung at the

2. Words by William Weston Patton, published in the *Chicago Tribune* on December 16, 1861, set to a folk music tune that probably originated in a regional militia. This version was very likely what Julia heard in Washington, D.C.

Republican and Democratic National Conventions, presidential inaugurations, even at the National Cathedral.[3]

But the story doesn't end there. Julia was through and through a mother, a fact reflected by her recalling the part about Jesus being born of woman while writing the lines not far from her own children that fateful night of its composition. One especially troubling characteristic of the Civil War is that for the first (and last) time in US history, major combat occurred between brothers of the very same family, and between fathers and their sons.

"The carnage of the Civil War sickened her and all but extinguished the holy fires of patriotism that once burned so passionately in her heart."

3. Alarmingly, it was sung at the Cathedral of Saints Peter and Paul (also known as the National Cathedral) just three days after the Twin Towers fell in 2001. Who might Christ and the serpent have represented for its hearers?

The war ended and life eventually returned to normal for most of the nation, but Julia was not done yet. The carnage of the Civil War sickened her and all but extinguished the holy fires of patriotism that once burned so passionately in her heart. In 1870, between the Civil War and the Franco-Prussian War, she issued the first statement in support of what would eventually become Mother's Day.

"Disarm! Disarm! The sword of murder is not the balance of justice."

In her proclamation, she calls addressees combatants, "each bearing after his own time the sacred impress, not of Caesar, but of God." She tells them: "Disarm! Disarm! The sword of murder is not the balance of justice." To women directly, she insists, "Our husbands will not come to us, reeking with carnage, for caresses and applause. Our sons shall not be taken from us to unlearn all that we have been able to teach them of charity, mercy, and patience."

★ ★ ★

For Julia, Caesar fell below God in the universal pecking order. Her ordering seemed to be God, family, country (in that order). In just nine years, she went from writing her battle hymn to laying the foundation for Mother's Day with her too often forgotten proclamation. She witnessed the supposed expediency and necessity of war—and was not convinced. Thankfully, she awoke from her "martial dreams."[4] God bless mothers like Julia.

4. Mark Twain, author of classic tales about Tom Sawyer and Huck Finn, was another writer who witnessed the carnage of the American Civil War. Many years later, he would write of "martial dreams" and the "holy fire of patriotism" being an ungodly motivation for war in his short story "The War Prayer" (http://warprayer.org).

Michael* and Joseph Hofer*

d. 1918

During the Reformation in sixteenth-century Europe, a movement occurred that is often overlooked and underappreciated. Distinct from Protestantism, the Radical Reformation was made up of Christians who took the Sermon on the Mount literally, including nonresistance to evil, refusal to take oaths, and living their faith simply. Adherents were referred to derogatorily as Anabaptists, which means "twice baptized," since they rejected infant baptism and would baptize adults a second time if they had been baptized at a younger age.

Three major Anabaptist groups have their roots in the Radical Reformation: Amish, Mennonites, and Hutterites. Today these groups constitute a large portion of what are called the historic peace churches, which also include the Society of Friends, (also known as Quakers, a group that broke off from the Church of England in the seventeenth century), the Church of the Brethren, and the Brethren in Christ Church. Anabaptists largely adhere to absolute Christian pacifism, the belief that all war and violence contradicts Scripture and

therefore is not acceptable for Christians to undertake. Fortunately for them, the United States protects the religious expression of its citizens,[1] and has allowed them to apply for exemption from service through conscientious objector status.

Just before the First World War, however, nationalism was high, and CO provisions were not well developed. German language classes were discontinued across the country, since it was the language of the enemy; people even called sauerkraut "liberty cabbage."[2] This did not bode well for one Anabaptist group, the Hutterites[3]—including the Hofer brothers of Rock Port, South Dakota.

Michael, Joseph, and David Hofer, along with Jacob Wipf, were drafted in May 1918 and sent by train to Camp Lewis, Washington, for training. On the train, in their black garb, thick German accents, and long (nearly Nazirite) hair and beards, they were ridiculed and threatened. Before they reached their destination, some recruits kidnapped them and forcibly shaved their heads and faces. But unlike Samson, the Lord did not leave them like the locks abandoned on the floor of the barbershop.[4] No, if anything, God strengthened them to persevere, to be strong and courageous in their coming trials.

1. For the most part, Christians who adhere to just war criteria are not legally permitted to exercise their conscience or respond in faith to their religious communities when a war is deemed unjust. A good example are Roman Catholic soldiers in the recent war in Iraq; the United States Council of Catholic Bishops declared the war to not meet the standards of just war doctrine, but that did not change the Uniform Code of Military Justice.
2. History often repeats itself; the term *freedom fries* might ring a bell for readers.
3. Hutterites had descended directly from Anabaptists who fled violent persecution in eastern Europe, and the Hofers' whole community spoke German fluently. The Hutterites, seeking refuge from required military service, immigrated to the United States at the personal invitation of President Ulysses S. Grant, settling largely in the Dakotas in the 1890s. The United States needed skilled farmers like the Hutterites after the devastation of the Civil War. Certainly, the nation collectively believed, war would not occur again very soon. But in less than one generation, America's own greatest war would be overshadowed by the First World War.
4. Judges 16:19.

It began with their refusal to sign their "Soldiers Statement," a document all recruits and draftees filled out with personal information. They feared that signing such a statement would imply their acceptance of the title of "soldier" for themselves; the military uniform represented idolatry to them. So in July of 1918, they were put in chains and taken to Alcatraz in California, where they were hung in chains by their wrists in the dungeon for fourteen days at a time. "High-cuffing" was when a man's hands were crossed and shackled and then looped over high bars in his cell so that only his toes touched the ground. Because they refused to be soldiers or to wear the uniform, they were kept naked for long stretches of time, in the coming winter of 1918. Every day, a crisp and neatly folded military uniform sat in their cells, free for the taking. All they were required to do was to relent in their stubborn faith. But they shared the heart of the early soldier saints: death before idolatry.

On November 11, the war ended, but not for the Hutterites. Alcatraz ceased to be a military prison, so they were taken to Fort Leavenworth, Kansas. In short order, exposure caught up with them and Michael and Joseph were hospitalized. David and Jacob were put in solitary confinement. Their families were alerted, but only in time to watch Joseph die from what the Army called pneumonia brought on by influenza. Michael had died the day prior and his body was waiting to be transported back to South Dakota. When his wife, Maria, insisted on seeing him, she lifted the coffin to see insult piled upon injury—he had been dressed in the military uniform he had refused for six months to wear.

"You'll see a subtle adornment beside their name, belying the great honor it bestows upon those who acquire it—'martyr.'"

Not long after this, President Woodrow Wilson outlawed the practice of high cuffing, calling it "barbarous and medieval." Following World War I, absolute pacifism was recognized and protected under military law, and conscientious objectors were allowed to perform noncombatant duties in uniform or, for a time, to be assigned to civilian public service camps.

If you visit the Rockport colony in South Dakota, you'll find a small cemetery filled with shoe box–sized grave markers with only names and dates adorning them, a reminder of the Hutterites' persistent simplicity. But if you find the site of Michael and Joseph Hofer, you'll see a subtle adornment beside their name, belying the great honor it bestows upon those who acquire it—"martyr."

★ ★ ★

Like Maximilian centuries before, the Hofers and Jacob Wipf refused to be measured for military garb, defying the military authorities who claimed power over those who pledged their first allegiance to the body of Christ. The four were subjected to military justice though they denied ever belonging to anyone but God. In denying the title of "soldier" Michael and Joseph were crowned with the title of "martyr." David and Jacob survived and were given no such recognition, unlike centuries before, when they would have been venerated and given the title "confessor," reserved for those who refused to recant in their stubborn faith.

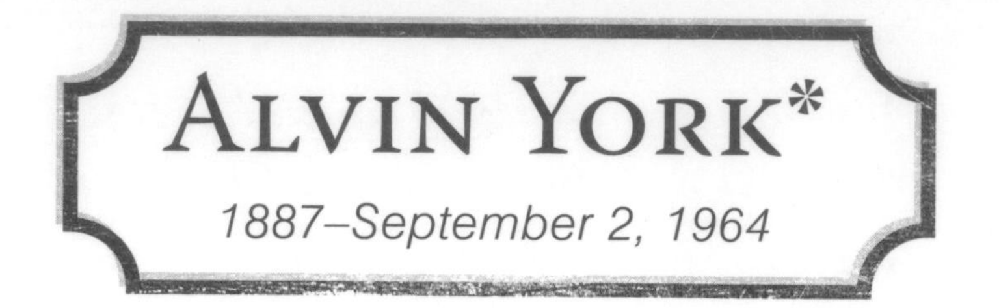

ALVIN YORK*

1887–September 2, 1964

Many people have heard the name Alvin York, the most decorated American soldier of World War I. The movie *Sergeant York*, based on Alvin's life, was the top-grossing film of 1941. During a battle in France, Alvin single-handedly captured 128 Germans in the face of heavy machine gun fire. For this and later actions, he received more than fifty awards, including the Congressional Medal of Honor. But in celebrating this courageous young man and American folk hero, we sometimes miss a few curious details.

Alvin York was a farm boy born and raised in the Valley of the Two Forks in rural Tennessee. A rabble-rouser in his youth, he would drink and brawl and curse most days and stay up late most nights. Not the most passive of souls, to be sure. But before long he found "that old time religion" and changed his ways.[1]

Alvin joined a small denomination known now as the Campbellites, with origins in the teachings of Thomas and Alexander Campbell.[2] He devoted himself to this church's teachings and pacifist doctrine in 1915, at twenty-seven years of age. Two years later, with World War I in full swing, he reluctantly registered for the draft. When asked, "Do you claim exemption from the draft?" he replied, "Yes. Don't want to fight." He would say later of his trepidation that "I was worried clean through. I didn't want to go and kill. I believed in my Bible."

---

1. See Jonathan H. Ebel, *Faith in the Fight: Religion and the American Soldier in the Great War* (Princeton University Press, 2010) for more background on the significance of religion in World War I.
2. The early forms of this tradition were vehemently pacifist. In fact, they broke from the Methodist Church because they felt the more mainstream denomination was too supportive of the Civil War.

He defended his right to refuse to bear arms several times, appealing the Selective Service's denial of the status at least three times. At the time, conscientious objector status was not the exemption from military service that COs currently can receive (thanks in part to the public outcry in response to episodes like the Hofer brothers of the last profile). Rather, COs in Alvin's time were guaranteed only that they would perform duties that the president of the United States deemed to be of a noncombatant nature. So Alvin began his training, waiting to hear where he would be assigned.

Alvin landed in the unit that a later generation would know as the Airborne All Americans, the 82nd Division. In a conversation behind closed doors, his commander cited Scripture left and right, giving Alvin plenty of food for thought for a short leave at home before shipping out to the front. While back at home, he took some time to pray at a nearby mountain range, not unlike John Vianney of Ars, during which he felt direction from God to trust in him and be not afraid.

Events that eventually would be listed in his Medal of Honor citation mostly occurred in France, where he effected the surrender of over 130 German soldiers. *Sergeant York*, the movie about his life, almost was not made, and Alvin refused to sell the rights to his story for over twenty years because of his religious concerns about Hollywood. In fact, documents passed between Warner Brothers producers reveal that they had an interest in using Alvin and his story to convince Americans to go to war. They even forged Alvin's signature in order to get Gary Cooper to play York on film. The memory and audacious character of Alvin was exploited for a political agenda, despite his best efforts.

The question remains: Where was God in all this? Alvin recalled to his division commander, "A higher power than man['s] power guided and watched over me and told me what to do."[3] That higher power did not whisper to him the mantra "Kill, kill, kill," which he might

3. Recounted in his war diary, dated January 1919.

have otherwise heard on the bayonet range back in training. Instead, he was moved to restraint, recalling later that "I didn't want to kill any more than I had to."[4] In the heat of the moment, York repeatedly yelled to the German machine gunners assaulting him, with a mere pistol in hand, to lay down their superior firepower.[5] The German officer in charge eventually surrendered his 132 men to York's care. When he came home, he didn't seek fame and fortune. Keen to return to his simple agricultural life in Tennessee, Alvin returned home and used his spare time and fame to advocate on behalf of local public education.

★ ★ ★

Like Maximilian or the Hofer brothers, some God-fearing soldiers are convicted to refrain from the military, while others are reassured that they are in God's protection. Which conviction is the rule and which is the exception is a subject of worthy debate, but debate is not what Alvin had in mind; he reported back for duty ready to serve God and country in the battlefields of Europe. The question of his service never seemed totally settled; he supported military interventions after World War I and World War II but wrestled with his own participation in war all the way to his deathbed, where he asked his son whether he could be forgiven for having killed all those men.[6]

"He wrestled with his own participation in war all the way to his deathbed"

4. Scribbled in his diary in an entry dated October 8, 1918.
5. The 1941 movie by Warner Brother omits this important element of the story. In the twenty-eight times actor Gary Cooper fires his weapon, not once does he call to the German forces to surrender. Bryan Fischer, writer of "The Feminization of the Medal of Honor," (see note 112, page 118) might like the Hollywood version more than he would York's version.
6. About five and a half minutes into *For God and Country* (Moda Entertainment), in a featurette about the movie based on his life, *Sergeant York; Two Disc Special Edition* (Burbank, CA: Warner, 2006), historian Michael Birdwell reflects on Alvin's deathbed remarks to his son George Edward, wondering "if God would forgive him for having killed those German soldiers in World War I."

CON
FLI
TE
DUTY
COURAGE

Thomas Bennett* *and* Joseph G. LaPointe*

d. 1969

The Congressional Medal of Honor is awarded by the president of the United States to members of the military. To receive it, one must be nominated either by their military chain of command or by a member of Congress, in recognition of personal acts of valor above and beyond the call of duty. And the awards have not always been given for acts of valor involving violence. Two Vietnam War recipients of the award in 1969 were, in fact, pacifists and had joined the military as noncombatants, because of their conscientious objection to violence:[1] Thomas Bennett and Joseph G. LaPointe. Joseph was working as a letter carrier when he was drafted. Thomas was in college and would have qualified for a deferment because of his studies. He was president of the Campus Ecumenical Council and by all accounts a devout man of faith. But as he watched the conflict escalate into full-blown war, he couldn't sit at home while other men his age were fighting far from home for principles he believed in and thrived upon.

---

1. The Selective Service recently has been revising its regulations regarding civilian and military noncombatant service. See http://www.army.mil/article/37811/selective-service-expands-alternatives-for-conscientious-objectors for more details on the recent development. I use the term *pacifist* here to mean "personally opposed to taking up arms in wartime," but not necessarily opposed to noncombatant service. "Pacifist" is usually taken to mean opposition to all participation in warfare. But even within some of the historic peace churches, those who call themselves pacifists have differed on whether their beliefs precluded noncombatant service in the military.

Both Thomas and Joseph were trained in Texas, at Fort Sam Houston, home to the Army Medical Education and Training Campus. Basic training for noncombatants was six weeks instead of eight, since they did not undergo weapons training. The men were not insulted or ridiculed, since cadre and staff in training units knew the soldiers would be tending to the wounded once "in-country." They were not afraid to enter combat settings; they only refused to kill.[2]

But the field medical specialty was not the only place conscientious objectors served. Beyond the military, they were also assigned to hospitals and mental institutions, providing needed care with little to no pay.[3] As troubling as it may sound, others volunteered for experiments to benefit the war effort. In at least one case, in 1944, volunteers from a civilian public service camp in Minnesota voluntarily starved themselves while journaling the experience. The war was nearing its end, and the Allies knew that millions in Europe were malnourished and would need dietary rehabilitation, but strategies were lacking. The Minnesota Starvation Recovery Experiment helped scientists, and the front line commanders who would implement their recommendations, provide better care to the millions of people soon to be liberated from the scourge of war and famine.

In 1969, the two soon-to-be Medal of Honor recipients served in different units: Thomas in the 25th "Tropic Lightning" Division and LaPointe in the 101st "Screamin' Eagles." Bennett arrived in-country in January 1969 and a sniper gunned him down as he attempted to tend a wounded comrade on February 11. Joseph had served in Vietnam since November 1968 and in July of the following year, he too was killed caring for the wounded. Twice wounded and using his body as a shield, he was finally taken by an enemy grenade on June 2,

2. There were many conscientious objectors to the war in Vietnam, though not all went on to serve as noncombatants. To hear their stories, see James W. Tollefson, *The Strength Not to Fight: Conscientious Objectors of the Vietnam War—In Their Own Words* (Boston: Little, Brown, 1993).

3. These COs, while also serving their country, refused noncombatant service in the military like that of Thomas and Joseph.

1969. Each of these young men embody the Christian maxim "For this faith, I will die, but I will not kill."

★ ★ ★

The memory of Thomas and Joseph reminds us that noncombatant soldiers are not cowards; they are capable of the same valor and courage that their compatriots display on the battlefield. One day, perhaps, noncombatants can again serve valiantly beside soldiers in uniform. Currently, that is not the case, at least in the United States, and it is a tragic reality that should trouble all Christians. Perhaps nations once again can honor and value the contributions of nonviolent men and women of faith who genuinely desire to serve their nations and their communities but who cannot bring themselves to rely on violence to do so.

VALOR

I really wanted to get done with college first. . . . I am in my reenlistment window and the Army is throwing big money at me to reenlist. I made a decision awhile ago that I was not going to do it. I plan on coming home. . . I want to pledge my allegiance to the cross and not the sword.

Clarence Jordan

1912–October 29, 1969

The American South in the 1930s was rife with racial tension. Less than one hundred years prior, after the Civil War, African Americans had their freedom from slavery but many were still brutally and violently oppressed. Segregation ruled: whites and blacks kept strictly separate company in schools, shops, public buildings, and churches. Even denominations remained unhealed from the wounds of generations of slavery and racism. The Baptist church split in two, its Southern body still refusing to condemn slavery.

One Southern Baptist, however, did not adhere to the same principles as his denomination. Clarence Jordan grew up in a church in which the white sheriff of his town could sing "Love Lifted Me" on Sunday, yet have beaten and tortured a black work camp prisoner the day before. As an undergraduate student of agriculture at the University of Georgia, he enrolled in the Reserve Officer Training Corps (ROTC). That meant that upon his graduation in 1933 he would be commissioned as a second lieutenant in the United States Army. He went through two years of additional classes on leadership and basic management just as ROTC cadets do in colleges nationwide to this day. After his second year, he participated in the summer boot camp that young cadets go through in preparation for entering a specialty. Clarence chose cavalry, perhaps in some small part because of the honored heritage of chivalric equestrian-bound soldiers before him.

America has been described as a huge melting pot, which means that "we the people" come from various backgrounds and cultures and races, "melted" together in one big diverse group. But like "we the

people," this is something that is always being revised and updated. In the South that Clarence grew up in, whites and blacks were segregated like oil and water. However, the military gave him a different picture: the possibility of racial reconciliation. While the United States military was, during Clarence's time, still segregated, it was nonetheless well ahead of society in general. African Americans were first commissioned as officers in World War I, not long before Clarence entered ROTC. By 1948, the military was officially desegregated by an executive order signed by President Eisenhower, nearly twenty years before the US Supreme Court decision *Brown v. Board of Education* integrated public schools and institutions.

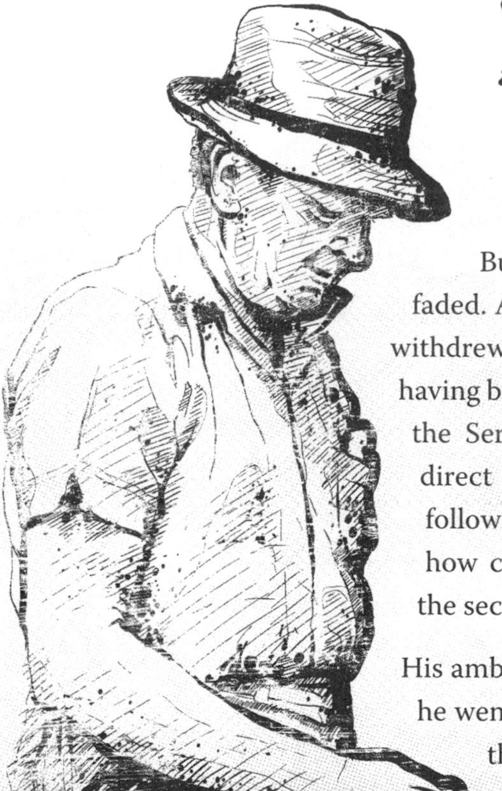

"The military gave him a different picture: the possibility of racial reconciliation."

But the stars in Clarence's eyes soon faded. After his boot camp experience, he withdrew from his ROTC scholarship, not having been able to square his training with the Sermon on the Mount, Jesus' most direct instructions for those who would follow him. As an officer in the military, how could he turn the other cheek, go the second mile, and bless his enemies?

His ambition for the gospel only grew, and he went on to earn a bachelor of divinity, the basic degree earned by church ministers, as well as a PhD in biblical Greek from a conservative Southern Baptist seminary.

He remained in Georgia, with all its struggles with racism, a struggle Clarence took up himself. He is famous for his Cotton Patch Gospel series; a common English version of the New Testament that used language Southern blacks and whites would be familiar with, reinterpreting Paul's letters for what they might say to Christians not in Ephesus or Rome, but Birmingham, Alabama, and Washington, D.C. He founded Koinonia Farms, a racially diverse and theologically progressive community that refused to let race have the last word, right in the heart of the South. Clarence helped put more color into a conversation that too often was polarized and dehumanizing, bringing in a racial tolerance he may have first experienced during his short time as a cadet.

★ ★ ★

Christians must be careful not to paint with too broad a brush when discerning their feelings about participating in the military. Military service is neither morally pristine nor absolutely reprehensible. Great strides for justice have begun within its ranks, but significant hurdles of conscience have needed to be overcome. The melting pot that we find ourselves in has often been tested in the military; often, in the throes of war, soldiers' preconceived notions about one another fall away and they see the brother or sister on their left and right as equally deserving of protection and respect—regardless of race or other social barriers.

John Weir Foote*

1904–May 2, 1988

Alvin York, Thomas Bennett, and Joseph LaPointe all were bestowed with the highest award their nation could give them, the Congressional Medal of Honor. Few people are surprised to find that frontline soldiers like York earned these "top of the line" medals. More folks will find it curious that conscientious objectors like Bennett and LaPointe would even be eligible for them. Most of us, however, might gasp in surprise to find that chaplains also are among its coveted ranks. But that has been the case in the United States since the conception of the award in 1861.[1]

In Britain, the highest award that can be given by Her Majesty is the Victoria Cross, awarded "for most conspicuous bravery or some daring or preeminent act of valour or self-sacrifice or extreme devotion to

1. See the section on chaplains for a list of Medal of Honor winners, beginning with John M. Whitehead in 1861, appendix 4 (page 190).

duty in the presence of the enemy." This award is often extended to soldiers of Commonwealth countries, former territories of the British Empire. Among these was John Weir Foote, a Presbyterian minister from Ontario who enlisted in the military at the ripe old age of thirty-six in 1939, at the outbreak of World War II.

In two years, John left home to participate in an ill-fated landing attempt in France. During the battle, he vigorously ministered to the wounded amid heavy enemy fire, upright and without cover for several hours, encouraging them, praying with them, reminding them by word and deed that they were not alone but that God was with them as they lay wounded or dying. Then, when the decision was made to retreat, he reluctantly boarded the landing craft that would take him back to safety, but he didn't stay for long. He thought of his fellow soldiers from the battle who were taken prisoner by the Nazis, who would without a doubt face cruel and unusual treatment at the hands of their enemy. So instead of motoring off to friendly territory, he jumped ship and forced his way to the German encampment and joined the Canadians bound for uncertain fates in an unforgiving collection of camps and prisons.[2]

2. According to the Geneva Conventions, chaplains are not technically prisoners of war. They are legally considered "detained persons" to be sent home, "unless ministering to POWs." The language makes me wonder if the conventions were worded in a specific way with Foote in mind, but there is no way to tell.

"As Christ's representative on earth, he knew that his place was with the oppressed, the threatened, and the imprisoned."

John spent the entire war, until his camp's liberation in 1945, as a prisoner of war.[3] As a man of God, he knew that God was with him and his men, even in war. As Christ's representative on earth, he knew that his place was with the oppressed, the threatened, and the imprisoned. His citizenship did not demand of him the four years he would spend in the harsh conditions that characterized German POW camps; he gave those years freely. His eyes were almost certainly on God in that moment when sailing back toward safety under his own flag, he turned to follow the cross of Christ—Emmanuel, God-with-us. He knew that if his men could not come to church, then church would come to them. And the gates of hell and Nazi prison camps would not prevail against him.

Upon John's return home to Canada at the end of the war, his unit was demobilized. From there, he went into politics for about ten years before he retired, following a series of heart attacks, in 1959. Before long, however, he returned to his military chaplaincy with the light infantry and was made an honorary officer. Like many veterans today, his sense of service to others was unquenchable, serving his country unarmed in war, in prison, and in politics, all within the frame of his Christian ministry. ☧

I [eventually] realized how incompatible my beliefs were with my intended profession as an Army Chaplain. ...what I've discovered throughout all of the fear, doubt, and shame is that I am coming out of a narrative that has so twisted the Lord's message that I am more and more galvanized by God's gracious love each day.

---

3. The third Geneva Convention was adopted in 1929, but largely updated after WWII. It is not clear that the legal protection would have been in place (and whether Foote could be legally called a POW at the time), but he was a prisoner during a time of war.

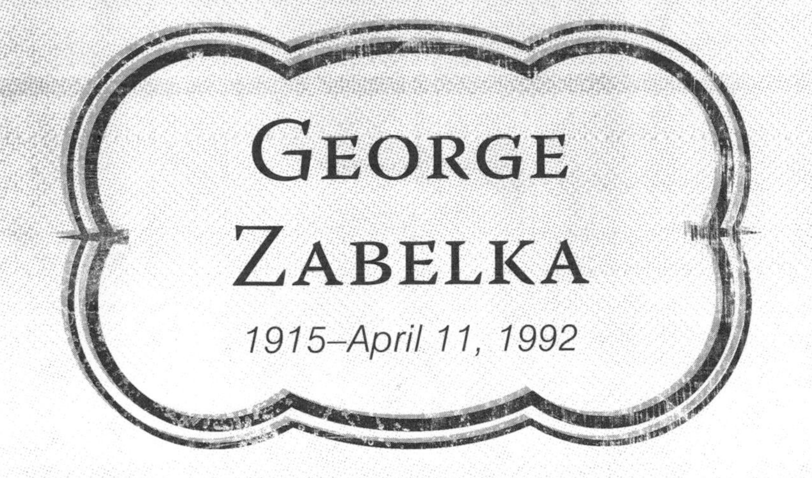

Six months to the day before the Japanese Imperial Army bombed a bustling military airfield in the American territory of Hawaii, George Zabelka entered the priesthood of the Roman Catholic Church. It was a church he later claimed was "heir to a Christianity that had for seventeen hundred years engaged in revenge, murder, torture, the pursuit of power, and prerogative of violence, all in the name of our Lord." But that day, June 7, 1941, he still had stars in his eyes for the church he had grown up with in Flint, Michigan, since 1915. He could don his vestments and not feel as though he was "a wolf in sheep's clothing."[1]

Father George's military career was short but significant. Two years after his ordination he entered the Air Force as a chaplain, and five years later, he would be discharged. Zabelka made it all the way to the rank of major within three years. Part of that advanced pace must have had to do with the great importance of where he was assigned—the 509th Composite Group on Tinian Island, which in the early '40s, was the busiest airfield on earth.

George spent his time doing what any Catholic chaplain did: hearing confessions, performing worship services, and listening to his troops. On August 6, 1945, a flight wing prepared for a mission to drop the

1. Quoted from "Blessing the Bombs," by George Zabelka, which Plough Publishing reprinted in 2011. Retrieved from http://www.plough.com/en/articles/2011/july/blessing-the-bombs.

"gimmick bomb," which they had heard of but knew very little about. So he did what any chaplain would; he blessed the crew, the aircraft, and its payload. Off they flew into infamy, destroying Hiroshima with the atomic bomb, and when they returned, the priest did as he always did—talked and listened, took confessions, and performed mass. Then three days later, the time came once more to repeat the bombing mission, this time in Nagasaki. So he did.

Saint Francis Xavier, an early Jesuit and companion to Ignatius of

What i love about chaplaincy is ministering where people work. It kills me seeing young people joining the Navy for healthcare, college opportunities, or a way to support their families. Part of my job is keep(ing) recruits in even though they may have reservations about staying in. I see the poor fighting rich peoples wars and it breaks my heart.

Loyola, had brought the Catholic faith to the Japanese centuries before. Nagasaki was the center of Catholicism in Japan; the Urakami Cathedral was the seat of the bishop's office and the largest church in the country. It was also ground zero for the second atomic mission. This bombing went against all military protocol; the imperial court of Japan was pleading for peace and offering to surrender with conditions. Furthermore, the weather on August 9th was bad and the mission was to be aborted if the clouds did not clear. Against all odds and against all morals, the bomb dropped onto the center of Catholic Christianity in Japan, flown by a Catholic pilot, and blessed by a Catholic chaplain.

"Nothing stood in the way of the bomb—not weather, and certainly not theology."

Nothing stood of the cathedral after detonation. Three orders of Japanese nuns were totally destroyed. The schools and hospitals that the diocese oversaw were all leveled. Nothing stood in the way of the bomb—not weather, and certainly not theology. Father George lamented that "The day-in-day-out operation of the state and the church between 1940 and 1945 spoke more clearly about Christian attitudes toward enemies and war than St. Augustine or St. Thomas Aquinas ever could." George was heir to a Christianity that had forgotten its own heritage. He only came to realize this years later, in 1972, when he began communicating with a pacifist named Father Emmanuel Charles McCarthy, founder of the Center for the Study of Nonviolence at Notre Dame and who himself had once been a cadet in the Reserve Officer Training Corps.

Fathers George and Charles traveled the world together, educating future generations on the virtues of nonviolence and preaching the gospel call to "love your enemies,"[2] and "turn the other cheek."[3]

2. Matthew 5:44; Luke 6:27; and Luke 6:35.
3. Matthew 5:39; the New Revised Standard Version actually reads "turn the other also" when you are struck on the right cheek, whereas Luke 6:29 uses "offer" instead of "turn."

George felt tortured by his uncritical acceptance of the status quo, of not having the moral and theological tools his office of chaplain required. He later traveled to Hiroshima and Nagasaki and saw first-hand the product of his and his nation's lack of moral clarity. But even the atom bomb could not ultimately destroy the church; there near ground zero, years after the twin days that live in theological infamy, he found communion with the very Japanese Christian community that suffered so severely for what he felt was his gravest mistake.

★ ★ ★

Sometimes, even if we think we know what we've gotten ourselves into, we don't have the context we otherwise might need. George had no idea that the men under his care were dropping the atom bomb. The entire crew likely had a very limited understanding of what they had unleashed until weeks, or even years, later. Furthermore, feedback from others in the 509th was varied; responses to our actions are never uniform. Not everyone in the division felt as guilty as their chaplain did. And yet, George's story challenges us to be honest about what we are doing and to understand the repercussions our actions have. Once he had the bird's eye view of what had happened, he was able to speak out—not to look down on others who participate, nor to be an arbiter of justice, but to offer a new expansive vision of peace. After recognizing his complicity in ushering in the nuclear age, he said that justice would not save; only "mercy is my salvation." God forbid that we pretend to be arbiters of justice; instead, let us pray to be made instruments of God's peace.

Francis Sampson

1913–January 28, 1996

One of three boys born to a South Dakota family, Francis Sampson was thoroughly Catholic, even graduating from Notre Dame University in 1937. After seminary in Minnesota, he was ordained a priest just months before Pearl Harbor was bombed in 1941. After a short stint teaching at a high school in Des Moines, Iowa, Father Francis was commissioned as a first lieutenant, becoming a chaplain in the 101 Airborne Division, the Screamin' Eagles.

On D-Day, Francis was the first chaplain to jump behind enemy lines, with the 501st Parachute Infantry Regiment. With a river serving as his landing area, he had to dive several times to retrieve his mass kit from the river bed, but he eventually joined the rest of his unit before becoming a German prisoner of war.

He was captured on two occasions. His first imprisonment occurred when Francis was tending to wounded American soldiers in a small French farmhouse.

When the Germans took the camp and enemy soldiers were wounded in the process, he treated them as well, showing as much concern for them as he did for his comrades. Despite this act of good faith, the Germans decided Francis needed to be executed, so they put him before a firing squad. In his memoir he recounts how, instead of reciting the act of contrition before his certain death, he uttered the prayer said before meals; "Bless us, our Lord, and these thy gifts, which we are about to receive through thy bounty through Christ our Lord, amen."

Miraculously, one of the German noncommissioned officers recognized Francis as a fellow Christian, stepped in on his behalf, and stayed his execution. Francis went right back to tending to wounded German soldiers until Americans recaptured the farmhouse.

Francis was captured again after his second combat jump, this time into Holland, in the midst of the Battle of the Bulge. Again he landed in water, this time in the moat of a medieval castle, and had to dive to retrieve his essential mass kit. Francis the POW was forced to march 185 miles to Germany, losing nearly a fifth of his body weight in the process. Insisting upon remaining with the enlisted men instead of going to the better-equipped officers' POW camp, Francis helped coordinate communication between advancing Allied troops and the prisoners of Stalag II-A.

The end of World War II came when the Russians liberated his camp and he returned to the States in October 1945. He went back to teaching in a small parish in Des Moines. He couldn't stay away from military chaplaincy for long, however, and reenlisted for the Korean War. His third combat jump was in 1950 with the 187th Airborne Infantry Regiment to rescue POWs being moved north toward China.

In 1967, Francis was appointed to the highest position he would hold—the chief of chaplains of the United States Army. Amid the antiwar activism of the 1960s and 1970s, he would often be asked how he,

as a man of the cloth, could support soldiering. Priests and soldiers, he said, "are both called to the identical things—that is—the preservation of peace, the establishment of justice when it has been lost, and the providing of security with protection for the weak and the innocent."[1]

Upon retiring from the military in 1971, Francis returned to simple parish life once again. He died of cancer at the age of eighty-three. The epitaph on his gravestone in Luverne, Minnesota, evokes another saintly Francis, the Italian, who also was familiar with the martial profession, yet prayed: "Lord make me an instrument of your peace." Francis Samson never carried a weapon in his entire twenty-nine-year military career, which spanned a world war and two conflicts in Southeast Asia.

★ ★ ★

The movie *Saving Private Ryan* was brutally honest in its depiction of World War II, helping society wrestle with what happened in that war more realistically. Disability claims for World War II vets in the VA claims systems doubled in the years following its release. Some speculate that this was because World War II vets no longer felt stigmatized for the service they rendered, which was often depicted too generically for them to feel comfortable admitting weakness. But Steven Spielberg based the story of Captain Miller and his platoon of Army Rangers on Father Francis Sampson, one chaplain without a single weapon in hand. After the landing at Normandy, a young soldier came to him trying to find the grave of one of his three brothers. So Father Francis grabbed a jeep and drove twenty miles behind enemy lines, only to discover the grave of a second brother. The third had been captured in the Pacific theater and was presumed dead. The surviving Nyland family attended a special private screening of the film prior to its public release and were said to have been quite satisfied with the end product.

1. See http://www.missioncapodanno.org.

Yevgeny Rodionov*

1977–May 23, 1996

The Union of Soviet Socialist Republics in the late twentieth century was not the best place for religious people. Communism reigned and Karl Marx, one of its founders, had famously suggested, "Religion is the opiate of the people." Christianity, like other religions, was a means to distract people from the struggle between the elite and the working class. While Christianity was not overtly outlawed, religious expressions were socially unacceptable, and could even be dangerous.

At a young age, Yevgeny "Evi" Rodionov's grandmother gave him a necklace adorned with a Russian Orthodox cross. Evi's mother, Lubov, was an atheist, and did everything she could to keep him from wearing it—not just because she felt it was a worthless charm, but also because it could endanger her young son. She worried less about the bullies at school than about the bullies among the Communist government authorities.

By the time he was eighteen years of age, the USSR had broken up, and the various former republics broke out in war. Evi was conscripted into the armed forces of Russia, but he only aspired to be a cook, nothing more. The seal of Christ he wore around his neck was not so big that his neck couldn't carry a dog tag or two. The heavy burden of soldiering was made light by Jesus' assistance. His call was not the

same that Maximilian of Tebessa heard in the third century, to refuse conscription, for not every call of Christ is the same.[1]

In his first year, he was deployed to fight in the warring republic of Chechnya, where there was little difference between a chef and a combatant. He was sent to the border area and assigned to a checkpoint with three other privates in the Russian forces. The war between Russia and Chechnya was, for the majority Muslim population of Chechnya, a *jihad*, a religious war and a just defense against an occupying force.

On February 13, 1996, the checkpoint at which Evi was stationed was approached by a truckload of Chechen soldiers. The platoon included a brigade general who was overseeing the transport of weapons. The four Russian soldiers were no match for the Chechens, so after a short fight, they were arrested and taken away.

When the young soldiers were discovered absent from their post, they were accused of desertion. A squad of Russian military police visited Evi's mother, asking for his whereabouts, thinking he had abandoned his duties out of fear. But Lubov knew her son was no coward.

Evi and his three comrades had not deserted at all, but had been taken to dank cells in a hidden location and high-cuffed like the Hofer brothers before him.[2] They were beaten severely and told that if they rejected Christianity, they would be let free. But Evi refused to take off

1. See page 67 for more about this third-century saint from North Africa.
2. See page 124 for more on the Hofer brothers and Jacob Wipf and their treatment during World War I.

the cross lying hidden next to his heart, a timeless symbol of tireless and unfailing faith. He felt the force of thousands of saints and martyrs who paved the way for him to hold fast to hope in Christ, even to death. He was beheaded on his nineteenth birthday on May 23, 1996.

As far as his unit was concerned, he had betrayed his country by deserting. That changed, however, after the Chechens approached Lubov, asking for money in exchange for the location of her son's corpse. Hoping against hope that it was a fraud, she knew the grave was her son's when she saw the silver cross Evi had always refused to remove. When the general involved in the capture was arrested, he confessed, but said Evi "had a choice to stay alive. He could have converted to Islam, but he did not agree to take his cross off."

The witness of her son's life and courageous death converted Lubov to Christianity. The story spread rapidly in the Russian Orthodox Church and religious art cropped up across Russia with his image, a large silver cross around his neck. Soldiers still kneel in the presence of the portraits, and the icon given to his mother by a famous iconographer is said to emit a pleasant odor. The Russian patriarchate has denied his cause for canonization, on the grounds that new martyrs have not been declared for some time, and that the church has never declared someone a saint who was killed in war.

★ ★ ★

Though Evi expressed it differently, his faith was as steadfast as innumerable soldier saints before him, like the third-century Maximilian, who was also beheaded for his convictions. Many could have easily spared themselves by simply making a show to the gods, by accommodating the powers that be. But Evi's faith, like theirs, welcomed death rather than submitting to idolatry. Christians are called to be steadfast not in their honor, but in their adherence to Christ, to the faith made possible and sustained by the blood of the martyrs and saints before them.

Tom Fox*

1951–March 9, 2006

Tom Fox made headlines in 2005 when he was taken hostage with three other men serving in Iraq. The men were not from the regular army. They were stationed in Iraq with Christian Peacemaker Teams (CPT), an organization inspired by Ron Sider's 1984 declaration that "Unless we . . . are ready to start to die by the thousands in dramatic vigorous new exploits for peace and justice, we should sadly confess that we never really meant . . . that the cross was an alternative to the sword."[1]

Christian Peacemaker Teams believe that Christians "can transform war and occupation, our own lives, and the wider Christian world through: the nonviolent power of God's truth, partnership with local peacemakers, and bold action." CPTers are known for their stubborn insistence on "getting in the way" of violence in conflict arenas where nobody wants to go: the drug wars in Columbia, the disputed and volatile Palestinian territories, and war-torn Iraq, where Tom found himself in 2005.[2]

Originally from Virginia, Tom directed the youth program at his local Quaker meeting in nearby Baltimore.[3] It was there, at the Religious

1. From his speech at the Mennonite World Conference in Strasbourg, France, in the summer of 1984, titled "God's Reconciling People." You can read it online at http://www.cpt .org/resources/writings/sider.
2. For more history on CPT, see *In Harm's Way: A History of Christian Peacemaker Teams*, by Kathleen Kern (Eugene, OR: Cascade, 2008).
3. Quakers do not refer to their congregations as "churches," but as "meetings."

Society of Friends meeting house, where he would enlist with CPT for work in Iraq and Palestine in 2004. He took CPT's training in nonviolence, and then was sent to work in Iraq.

On November 25, 2005, he was abducted along with three other CPTers: Englishman Norman Kember and Canadians James Loney and Harmeet Singh Sooden. Their work, however, continued into captivity as they refused to endorse violence and submitted to CPT's policy of not paying ransoms or calling for a military rescue. They took seriously Jesus' call to love their enemies, even those who would do them harm.

Violent harm was precisely what the kidnappers, the Swords of Righteousness Brigade, intended. Just over three months into the ordeal, on March 9, 2006, local residents in Baghdad found Tom's body near a railroad, his hands bound, a bullet each to his head and his chest. They alerted coalition forces, seeing that the he was obviously not an Iraqi. The following day, military officials claimed there were signs of torture, though no evidence was provided.

Back home, CPT refused to match the violence of the kidnappers, quoting Tom himself, who had said, "We reject violence to punish . . . We forgive those who consider us their enemies." Leaders of CPT also insisted publically that the hostages' explicit requests, including that military intervention not be employed in their rescue, be honored.[4]

On March 23, a task force made up of various international military units orchestrated the rescue of the hostages from the Mansour neighborhood of Baghdad. A self-identified leader of the Swords of Righteousness group had been captured just prior, and gave the location of the hostages in exchange for his own release, as well as permission to phone his subordinates to warn them to evacuate. The military

4. Tom Fox's blog was left online after his death and can be read at http://waitinginthelight.blogspot.com.

agreed and kept their promise to the leader. Meanwhile, Christian Peacemaker Teams had not coordinated with the Royal Canadian Mounted Police, the British Special Air Service, the American Special Forces, or any of the other elite military units. They were, after all, trying to honor the wishes of their own members. In the aftermath, CPT was accused of not showing gratitude to the military forces for the rescue that they had performed.[5]

That it was the lone American who was executed might tell us something about the deep-seated anger toward the United States for leading the 2003 invading forces. The Canadian and British hostages, by contrast, were never harmed, and were even allowed to exercise and receive medical attention during their captivity. They were in good medical condition upon their safe return.

Tom's death may also have been related to his military record. Before he had become a CPTer, he had retired from the United States Marines after twenty years of service in the Marines' marching band. His musical role, however, might have been of little significance to people who knew mostly the violence that greeted them late at night when the Marines brandished their rifles and shouted commands in a language few Iraqis could speak fluently.

Tom's daughter reflected glowingly on her dad's service, remarking that his principles and convictions about the military prevented him from enjoying the perks of the Marines, including discounts he might have received. His service as a CPT volunteer was not about rewards and glory—it was about sacrificial work for peace.

5. The language of "rescue" was used in the original media reports in Britain, Canada, and the United States. CPT itself, however, had a policy of not seeking military rescue.

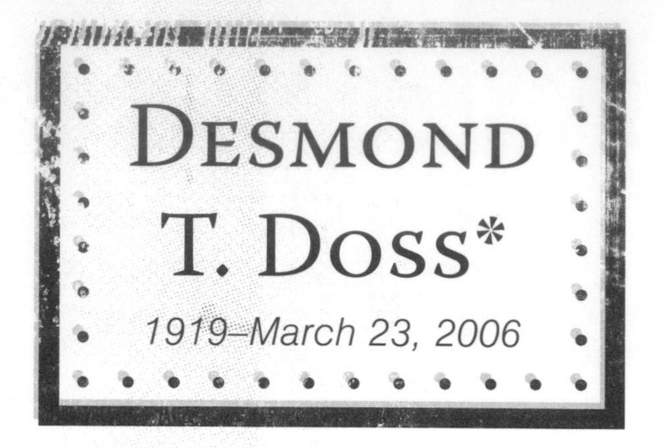

Desmond T. Doss*

1919–March 23, 2006

Desmond was a country boy, born and raised near the Washington and Jefferson national forests in Virginia, outside his hometown of Lynchburg. As a youth, he once walked several miles to donate blood to a girl he had never met, who had been in an accident. Two days later, he made the walk again for another unknown recipient, foreshadowing a heart for service that would continue to save lives many years later.

Working in a naval shipyard during the outbreak of World War II, he had a safe deferment from the draft, but he wanted to serve his country. The problem was that as a Seventh Day Adventist, he also served a God who reminded young Desmond, "Thou shalt not kill."[1] A simple man, he didn't parse the Hebrew or delve into complex equations justifying war; he just wanted to do the right thing. Seventh Day Adventists rest and worship on Saturday instead of Sunday and have their roots in New England pacifism of the 1860s, so Desmond's proactive pursuit of national service in the military made him a walking paradox: a patriot pacifist.

As soon as he got to basic training, the threats and insults began when his comrades watched him carry on without the obligatory firearm and noticed that he was exempt from duty on Saturdays. One enlistee

---

1. The sixth of the Ten Commandments, King James Version. Contrary to common misconceptions, the distinction between "killing" and "murder" does not exist in the original Hebrew in the same way it does in English.

told Desmond he would personally kill him when they got overseas. Because he insisted upon resting on the seventh day, Saturday,[2] his commander repeatedly tried to have him involuntarily discharged. Private Doss would have none of that, bouncing from platoon to platoon until he landed in a medical attachment. He would repair, not inflict, the wounds of war, even as they occurred around him.

Escaping a forcible discharge disguised by language accusing him of mental instability (a common accusation made against patriot pacifists), he went off to combat with the 307th Infantry, 77th Infantry Division. In the summer of 1944, seeing combat first in Guam and then in the Philippines, Doss was awarded the Bronze Star. His greatest accomplishment would come the following spring, as he accompanied his unit to Okinawa, Japan, to support combat operations there, in a battle that came to be known as Hacksaw Ridge.

Upon that treacherous ridge Desmond earned America's highest award, the Congressional Medal of Honor. On that day, May 5th, 1945, his citation credits him with the rescue of innumerable comrades, under heavy direct fire from enemy forces. Perhaps more noteworthy was that his heroism, which shone so brightly, took place on a Saturday. In explaining himself he revealed a hint of prophetic insight, saying, "Even Christ healed on the Sabbath."[3]

2. Seventh Day Adventists also adhere strongly to the fourth commandment: to remember the Sabbath and keep it holy.

3. Quoted from Richard Goldstein's obituary of Doss in the *New York Times*, "Desmond T. Doss, 87, Heroic War Objector, Dies." From http://www.nytimes.com/2006/03/25/national/25doss.html?_r=0, accessed June 3, 2013.

As a medic, he was trained to treat the least wounded first, a reversal of traditional triage. But Desmond never left somebody simply because they were unresponsive. That day, with no regard to his personal safety, Desmond guided the ambulatory, carried the wounded, and dragged the unconscious across fields of bullets flying like swarms of angry hornets. With each wounded friend he dragged from harm, he would repeat, "Dear God, just let me get one more." He would repeat that prayer seventy-four times before allowing himself his Sabbath rest. The official report, in attempting to explain the unfathomable success at Hacksaw Ridge, cites the only reasonable answer Desmond's commander could conjure up: "Doss prayed!"

Weeks after the daring rescue, he was injured by Japanese fire. For five hours he self-administered treatment for numerous shrapnel wounds to his torso and legs, concerned for the safety of other medics who would have had to emerge from cover to help him. Later, as he was litter-carried to safety, he jumped off the stretcher to assist other medics tending to a more seriously injured solider. For his audacity, he was again injured by enemy fire, suffering a compound fracture to his arm. Again, hoping to conserve other medics' supplies, he jerry-rigged a sling with junk he found around him at the time. Without much choice, and needing a slender, stiff object to set his arm, he used a discarded rifle as his splint. It was the only time he ever compromised his conviction against handling weapons.

★ ★ ★

Desmond knew what it was to honor the orders of the officers appointed above him while seeking, ultimately, to obey God. His witness stands as a reminder of our call to work within the structures of this world to recklessly advance God's realm. Never promising to be an easy task, it is nonetheless a worthy pursuit. Desmond was certain his actions were accompanied by divine providence. "All the glory should go to God," he said. "No telling how many times the Lord has spared my life."

Bill Mahedy

1936–July 20, 2011

In the 1960s and 1970s many young men of faith were drafted into the conflict in Southeast Asia without being granted special accommodations for their convictions against the use of violence, whether being allowed not to serve at all, or to serve in noncombatant roles such as a medic. The Selective Service and local draft boards applied draft laws inconsistently for religious exemptions and considerations. Stories abound of Christians from as diverse traditions as Catholics to Eastern Orthodox to Protestant being told that their traditions were not covered under the same protections given to people of Anabaptist, Quaker, and other historic peace churches.[1]

Furthermore, the social and cultural revolution around women's rights and protections for minorities, as well as the American churches' shortcomings in those areas, led to significant disaffections in US religious life. Many left the church for ecclesial and political reasons.[2]

---

1. Even the Church of the Brethren, an Anabaptist offshoot and a historic peace church, experienced denials of conscientious objection. One church I attended briefly in Hawaii had lost all affiliation with the peace tradition of their origins, due in large part to their proximity to the military affairs in Honolulu in the '60s. Many of the stories I have in mind were passed to me in personal conversation, as consolidating and recording the various practices of regional draft boards might be nearly impossible. Anyone interested in American history and want a book idea?
2. Theologian James McClendon suggests that this period marked a theological crisis from which America is still recovering. The disenfranchisement of Christians calls the church to look for theology within the biographies of individuals like Martin Luther King Jr., Dag Hammarskjold, Clarence Jordan, and others. See McClendon's book *Biography as Theology; How Life Stories Can Remake Today's Theology* (Eugene, OR: Wipf & Stock, 2002).

When I was growing up we went back and forth betwee a lot of churches, and then my parents dropped out of **the church all together.** They'd had a lot of painful experiences with unloving people. Somewhere along the li I think I lost my **faith** in **God** though and put my faith in **community** .. and then community let me down and I spent a long time just being empty

Many military enlistees who wanted to be conscientious objectors were left to theologically fend for themselves before draft boards, which had the power to send them to war without an ounce of theological oversight from local or national church entities. When they walked reluctantly off to war, they frequently turned their backs on the churches without looking back, feeling abandoned in their hour of need. God developed a reputation for being absent without leave.

Bill Mahedy entered the priesthood in 1958, not long before the peak of this turmoil. Few priests were tasked with shepherding the flock of Christians being sent to war, especially since this war in Vietnam seemed to violate the papal overtures in a 1963 document titled *Pacem in Terris*, "Peace on Earth." Bill entered the army as a Catholic chaplain and went to Vietnam to minister to soldiers getting hurt and killed there. He recalls that the preeminent question being asked by soldiers was "Where is God?" Where was God's church when men were called to serve against their will and against their conscience? Where were chaplains willing to hear the horror the men had to absorb on their own and find meaning for? To them, far from home and

forced into dire circumstances, there was no God, no meaning. "It don't mean nothin'" became their refrain.

The stories broke Bill's heart. He saw a sober truth in their words: churches had failed soldiers and had thus lost moral and spiritual authority in their lives. Even chaplains refused to see the crisis of faith in returning soldiers. Bill likened returning war veterans to the prophets of old—rejected by the people whom they sought to serve. In his 1984 reflections on his experience in Vietnam, he wrote, "The man who returns from combat and says, 'I am an animal,' knows a certain truth about himself. The person who taunts him or cannot bear to hear his story is simply hiding from the truth."[3] He called the post-Vietnam American experience an unacknowledged hypocrisy that only the veterans and those who dared to know them saw clearly.

Bill left the Catholic Church when he fell in love, but remained a priest. As an Episcopal clergyman, he worked tirelessly to improve the welfare of the Vietnam veteran community. Before the Veterans Affairs and the American Psychological Association recognized post-traumatic stress disorder, he and others made sure it eventually would be recognized. Bill was among a small group of energetic and creative activists who reformed the way the VA treated its patients and created the off-site Vet Centers that move treatment out of the white-walled confines of regional medical centers and into local communities where they are needed.[4]

---

3. *Out of the Night: The Spiritual Journey of Vietnam Vets* (Knoxville, TN: Radix, 2004), 57.
4. Scott, Wilbur. *Vietnam Veterans Since the War: The Politics of PTSD, Agent Orange, and the National Memorial* (Norman, OK: University of Oklahoma, 2004).

"Lord, may we who have been scarred by war be reconciled to each other, to our enemies, and to you."

In our generation, some have begun a movement to recognize what is being called "moral injury,"[5] building upon many of the concepts shared with PTSD. Bill wrote decades ago about the moral strain and pain experienced by our fighting men and women, even in causes the church might consider just. His heart was always for his comrades, especially their spiritual journey toward healing. He wrote liturgies specifically for veterans coming home trying to find meaning in the midst of the chaos that rages in their hearts and minds. His prayer for veterans was to be "delivered from the scourge of war."

★ ★ ★

Lord, may we who have been scarred by war be reconciled to each other, to our enemies, and to you. May we become peacemakers in all that we do. May we always be agents and instruments of your peace. Grant to those who are as yet untouched by war the great gift of continued freedom from the terrible agonies of armed conflict. We ask this through Jesus Christ, your Son, our Lord. Amen.[6]

5. These efforts have culminated in a Soul Repair Center at Brite Divinity School in Fort Worth, Texas. See www.britesoulrepair.org and Rita Brock and Gabriella Lettini, *Soul Repair: Recovering from Moral Injury after War* (Boston, MA: Beacon, 2012).
6. William P. Mahedy, *Out of the Night: The Spiritual Journey of Vietnam Vets* (Knoxville, TN: Radix Press, 2004), 241.

JOSHUA CASTEEL

1979–August 25, 2012

In the second year of the American occupation of Iraq, prison guards in the now-infamous Abu Ghraib prison were accused of abusing and humiliating prisoners of war being held there. The image of naked men in piles on the floor, one with a dog's leash around his neck, shocked many around the world. Another of a man covered in a black hood, arms stretched as wide as Christ's cross, standing on a box of food with wires attached to his fingers, quickly became iconic of American presence in the Middle East.

Not long after the images made the evening news, Joshua Casteel was stationed at that same prison as an interrogator and Arabic linguist. His job gave him access to Arab jihadists, soldiers of another faith, Islam. The Arabic word for a just warrior is *mujahid*, and its plural form is *mujahedeen*. The mujahedeen often see their fight as being as just as many Christian soldiers do. Just as faithful Christian warriors might be required to kill in the pursuit of justice, *mujahedeen*, or *jihadists*, see the violence they commit as attempting to restore justice and provide for a lasting peace.

Joshua found this out the hard way when he began interrogating one *mujahid*. Joshua was a devout Christian, face to face with one of the men he was questioning—another, equally devoted, warrior of *Allah* (the Arabic word for God). Like those who belong to Christian

religious orders and pray the "the liturgy of the hours," his Muslim enemy was called to prayer five times a day.

Joshua discovered, painfully at times, that we are not so different from our enemies. Sometimes we have different words for the same things. We fight for what we think is right, just as our enemies often fight for what they genuinely feel to be a just cause. The supposed certainty of Joshua's cause caused him significant doubt. Less than two months after arriving in Iraq, he wrote, "As long as I sit in my current seat of authority [over Muslim just warriors], with a weapon strapped across my back, the moral high ground seems somewhat clouded."[1]

His political doubts began piling up, so he went to speak with a chaplain, who encouraged him to nurture the ruthlessness and belligerence a US Army interrogator needed. His task, after all, was to exploit the anxieties, weaknesses, and fears of Iraqi detainees to gain intelligence. According to Joshua, this chaplain "did not pray me to the gospel. He prayed me back to combat."

The contradiction could not be starker, and the episode paved the way for Joshua to hear the gospel, instead, out of the mouth of a *mujahedeen*, with whom Joshua (quite unprofessionally) had an unwitting heart-to-heart conversation on October 18, 2004.

His interviewee asked him pointedly, "Your Lord [Jesus], our prophet Isa, tells you to turn the other cheek, to love those who hate you. Why do you not do this?" From the most

1. Joshua Casteel, *Letters from Abu Ghraib* (Ithaca, NY: Essay Press, 2008), 19.

unexpected places, from Jesus in one of his most surprising disguises, the Word of God came to Joshua through the mouth of his enemy.

> *"From the most unexpected places, from Jesus in one of his most surprising disguises, the Word of God came to Joshua through the mouth of his enemy."*

From there, his spirit only grew stronger. Two weeks later, he spoke with his commander about his intention to file for discharge as a conscientious objector. The commander graciously supported him in his decision, and Joshua was discharged honorably in May 2005. Soon after, he began speaking out actively in favor of Christian peacemaking.

One week before Veterans Day in 2011,[2] Joshua was diagnosed with stage four cancer in his lungs, spine, and other vital organs. In Iraq, he had overseen waste disposal at Abu Ghraib, where they burned everything from classified documents to computers and excess chemicals. During his extensive treatment, he testified repeatedly that he believed it was the burn pits he oversaw that caused him, at just thirty-one years old, to contract such a severe case of cancer. He passed away in

---

2. Joshua was scheduled to present on "The Arts, Warfare, and Social Post-trauma" at an event organized by students at Duke University Divinity School, called After the Yellow Ribbon—a resource for vets and others to think theologically about experiences of war. We dedicated the event to him. The sessions are available at: http://itunes.apple.com/us/itunes-u/milites-christi/id477245098.

August 2012, leaving behind his mother and two sisters to receive for him the prestigious Saint Marcellus Award from the Catholic Peace Fellowship at the basilica at the University of Notre Dame.

★ ★ ★

When I know not what I do, God grant me the grace to forgive, so that I might in turn remember how I, too, once was forgiven. But every time I kneel before the cross, praying both for them and more so for myself, I ask God to give me the time when I might put down my own sword, put down this seat of authority, and pick up the Eucharist. How much I would rather be a priest to people than to be their accuser. I am dying of self-absorption, convinced of my own myths of importance. Forgive my own conflicting allegiances and doubt. God forgive my lack of faith, my unwillingness to believe in Your redemption, and my efforts to conjure my own. God grant me wisdom, compassion, and a genuine desire for Truth that knows no national patronage.

— Joshua Casteel[3] ☧

GRANT ME GRACE

3. The words of this prayer are taken directly from Joshua's book *Letters from Abu Ghraib* (Ithaca, NY: Essay Press, 2008).

John M. Perkins

1930–present

Like Clarence Jordan before him, John M. Perkins saw firsthand the brutality of racism in the South, but for John it was seen from the eyes of the oppressed, for John is black. He was born a sharecropper's son in Mississippi in June 1930. In 1946, a white deputy sheriff killed his older brother Clyde, who had recently returned from World War II with a Purple Heart. In John's words, "He had come home safe from the white man's war only to be shot down six months later by a white man in his own hometown."[1] Like many black soldiers, upon coming home he found that the same freedom he fought for in Europe and the Pacific had gone AWOL in his own front yard.

On the battlefield of "the good war," black and white soldiers regularly fought valiantly alongside one another. The cause was clear even if the victory was not always so sure. To overcome evil, soldiers had to put their own evils aside. As the war ended, however, Southern blacks were marginalized and maltreated the moment their feet touched home soil. Black soldiers often had exceptional difficulty gaining access to the Servicemen's Readjustment Act of 1944, or "GI Bill," that provided education benefits to veterans. Even Japanese American soldiers, who

---

1. John M. Perkins, *Let Justice Roll Down* (Ventura, CA: Regal, 1976), 22.

had been met with so much suspicion after Pearl Harbor that thousands had been interned in camps for no reason other than their race, did not appear to have the same problems gaining their veterans benefits as did blacks in the South. Legally mandated benefits—low-cost mortgages, business loans, tuition assistance, living expenses, and unemployment compensation—were repeatedly denied or delayed to black soldiers.

We sometimes forget that the civil rights movement of the '60s would likely never have happened if not for the black soldiers coming home from World War II. The irony of having one standard on the battlefield and a different one at home laid the groundwork for the broader African American civilian population's dissent to finally boil over in the civil rights movement fifteen years after the war.

After his brother Clyde's murder in 1947, John fled racism in the South and headed to California. Soon he enlisted for military service, evidently maintaining some level of respect for the Army that bestowed the awards Clyde had received. But in basic combat training, "All they did was teach us to kill, kill, kill."[2] He served discreetly in Japan for three years during the Korean War and returned to California when his service expired in 1953.

"He encouraged whites and blacks alike to follow him to the freedom Christ offered, in which there were no racial divides."

After his son invited him to Sunday school, John became a born-again Christian. Then, persuaded by the Spirit to return in 1960 to his hometown in Mississippi, he became a civil rights activist, convinced his community needed to be brought back to Jesus. Evangelicals cite John as the father of racial reconciliation for his work in California

2. Dr. Perkins expressed this in an exchange with me in the summer of 2011 when I was a volunteer for the Summer Institute, a conference held every year through Duke's Center for Reconciliation.

labor unions and his decision to return to the Deep South despite the racism to which he knew he was returning. Before long, his children were among the first black students admitted to the formerly all-white public schools in his home county of Simpson, Mississippi. There, in the midst of segregated schools and churches, he spoke and wrote courageously, knowing that silence was not an option. Writing many books despite only having achieved a third grade education, he shared his story of pain with deep conviction but also with profound grace toward the white men and women who often publicly attacked and humiliated him. He encouraged whites and blacks alike to follow him to the freedom Christ offered, in which there were no racial divides.

As an ambassador of Christ, John knew that reconciliation would be painful and offensive: how dare he suggest that, though we are entitled to remain in anger, God calls us to overcome fear by God's love? As a veteran, he appreciated that a battle is indeed taking place, that a force exists worth fighting for. "The founding fathers had the idea that they were supposed to reflect the Kingdom of God, and as a result made one nation under God with liberty and justice for all."[3] But our fight is not to win, but to love. It is the ultimate fight, the final fight. While much of the country was up in arms about the Vietnam War, John was slowly and patiently building an army of reconcilers, developing communities of love, communities fighting the good fight of the faith.

★ ★ ★

Soldiers provide a unique window into the difficulty of forgiving, of letting go of all our good reasons to hold our hands in fists. History has shown us that our enemies have theirs clenched just as tightly as we do. Jesus speaks most directly of soldiers when he begs God to "forgive them, for they do not know what they are doing"—those who detained, mocked, beat, and executed him. To be a Christian is to believe that the words "forgive them"[4] are as powerful and poignant as "Let there be light."[5] In reconciling our theology and our faith with military service, we come closer to the kingdom of God. In learning of our reconciliation with God, we are enabled to reconcile with our enemies, and with all those people who, despite their own efforts, are naked, addicted, homeless, hungry, thirsty, and locked up.

3. From a lecture he gave at Belhaven University on March 27, 2012, available online at http://blogs.belhaven.edu/chapel/2012/03/27/dr-john-perkins-founder-perkins-foundation-for-reconciliation-and-development-3-27-2012/.
4. Luke 23:34.
5. Genesis 1:3.

Charles Liteky*

1931–present

On a cold December morning in 1967 in Vietnam, a young chaplain found himself on a search and destroy mission with the 12th Infantry Regiment. Coming under fire from a larger-than-expected enemy contingent, Father Angelo "Charles" Liteky was soon wounded in the neck and the foot. That didn't stop him, however, from quick action. When he saw two men lying wounded in the mud near an enemy machine gun nest, he dragged them to the safety of a landing zone several hundred meters away. Then he went back for more. Twenty more, to be exact.[1] He directed the ambulatory wounded toward the landing zone at which he had established a rally point.

Some of the unconscious wounded men he came across were too heavy to carry or drag. Instead, he low-crawled with them the distance to the LZ and made sure they were seen by one of the medics there. The enemy saw this going on and directed heavy fire in his direction, but beyond the initial foot and neck wound, he never saw a

1. Charles's story has much in common with the Vietnam portion of the story of Forrest Gump; both are wounded while dragging comrades to an aide station and both are involved in the antiwar movement, even after being awarded their medals. Michael Gallagher of the *Los Angeles Times* was among the first to note the similarities; see http://articles.latimes.com/1995-07-09/opinion/op 22018_1_vietnam-war.

scratch in the hours-long firefight. At one point he saw a loaded US machine gun lying on the battlefield, waiting to be put to use. Father Charles stared at it, removing his gaze and returning to work only after hearing a voice in his head say, "If they should find a priest dead on the battlefield today, they will not find in his hands a weapon of this world."

His courage under fire inspired his unit to rally, and it successfully suppressed enemy fire, gaining them a respite while the wounded were evacuated. Overnight, while waiting for their own exfiltration, Father Charles continued to inspire the men, going up and down the line of fire telling them to remain strong, persevering until morning light and a successful extraction of all friendlies, wounded included. His persistence in the battle, and his perseverance while waiting for the unit's return to safety gained him America's highest honor: the Congressional Medal of Honor. President Lyndon B. Johnson would place the award around his neck in November 1968.

In 1971, Father Charles's military service ended. He could have gone on to live the quiet life of a hero. But his service to the church and to the world was not over. During the war, the church had difficulty offering a prophetic challenge to the zeal with which the United States went to war. In 1975, Charles left the Roman Catholic priesthood and began involving himself heavily in movements opposing US policies in Central America. In 1986, he became the first Medal of Honor recipient to return his award, sending it in an envelope addressed to President Reagan in protest of the aid his administration was giving to Nicaraguan Contras. He served a six-month jail sentence for gaining access to Georgia's School of the Americas and spilling blood over display cases and pictures that served as a kind of hall of fame. A second sentence, this time for one year, came in 2000 for trespassing on government property at Fort Benning, Georgia, protesting the same school. Of his sentence, he said:

> I consider it an honor to be going to prison as a result of an act of conscience in response to a moral imperative that impelled and obligated me to speak for voices silenced by graduates of the School of the Americas, a military institution that has brought shame to our country and the US Army.[2]

★ ★ ★

Charles, a former priest and Medal of Honor recipient, knew what courage and conscience required. Following our God-given consciences can at times be physically threatening, and at other times politically threatening. He was prepared to sacrifice his body in Vietnam and ended sacrificing his Medal of Honor back in the safety of home.

2. In "Army Hero Turned Activist Headed to Prison for Trespassing" by Michael Taylor, *San Francisco Chronicle*, June 9, 2000.

Camilo Mejía

1975–present

Nicaragua in the mid '70s was a violent and unpredictable place, ravaged by a civil war between the dictatorial Somoza regime and revolutionaries calling themselves Sandinistas. Carlos Mejía Godoy was a Roman Catholic seminary student who studied with the Jesuits, but who left his studies to take part in the fight against the unjust authority exercised by Somoza. A musician at heart, Carlos wrote a melody styled after the Catholic mass and called it the "Misa Campesina" (People's Mass). He wrote other songs that put to music instructions on how to assemble and use rifles recovered by the Sandinistas after battles.

Into this maelstrom a young boy was born into the Mejía family. He was named Camilo, after Camilo Torres, a liberation theologian and revolutionary priest. Camilo's mother and father did not stay together, and he eventually emigrated to the United States. Like his father, he received a Jesuit education, earning decent grades and thirsting for higher education. In 1995, he signed up with the Florida National Guard in order to pay for tuition at the University of Miami. A recruiter told him that, as a Guardsman in a time of peace, he would likely never see combat. Guardsmen remain in the state to assist in humanitarian efforts like floods and hurricanes. They report to the governor, not the president. Or so he was led to believe.

But the recruiter proved to be wildly off mark. In the wake of 9/11 and an initial invasion of Afghanistan, the United States was poised to start a second war, this time in Iraq. Camilo was called up for active duty, despite his reservations about the legitimacy of the war. He knew that the Vatican had declared that any aggression in Iraq would not satisfy the centuries-old doctrine of "just war," a set of four criteria to guide the global Roman Catholic Church in recognizing when a proposed war would be considered just:

1. The damage inflicted by the aggressor on the nation or community of nations must be lasting, grave, and certain.
2. There must be serious prospects of success.
3. All other means of putting an end to the problem must have been shown to be impractical or ineffective.
4. The use of arms must not produce evils and disorders graver than the evil to be eliminated.

> The evaluation of these conditions for moral legitimacy belongs to the prudential judgment of those who have responsibility for the common good.[1]

---

1. *The Catechism of the Catholic Church* lays the foundation for Catholic doctrine and belief. Just war criteria can be found in paragraph #2309, Section III ("Safeguarding Peace"), Article V ("The Fifth Commandment"). Page numbers vary by edition, but I cover just war in appendix 8.

Camilo deployed, hoping to do his time and come home. But in his first six months, he witnessed grave sins that he could not ignore, including the use of torturous "enhanced interrogation measures."[2] He could not be party to what he saw, so when he was given time to go home, he stayed there. He went into hiding for a time, preparing a belated conscientious objector application, in which he cited Catholic just war doctrine regarding moral conscience. In his application he cited another paragraph from the catechism that describes the conscience as "the soft, still whisper of God" within each believer where they are "alone with God, whose voice echoes in their depths."[3]

Having bid too little too late, however, he was court-martialed, reduced in rank, and imprisoned. His sentence included his being discharged for bad conduct. At the end of his trial, before he went to the brig, he said, "Refusing and resisting this war was my moral duty, a moral duty that called me to take principled action." Like John of Ars before him, his conscience led him to desert the military, only to become something much greater thereafter, including being interviewed by Dan Rather and being labeled a prisoner of conscience by Amnesty International. Ironically, he was released early from his sentence for good conduct.

Like his father before him, Camilo is diligently unorthodox, a thoughtful, provocative, and subversive servant to the church. Soldier saints often are, as Francis of Assisi found himself frequently "outside the bounds of orthodoxy."[4]

---

2. As torturous as they were, not all techniques compare to the interrogation some soldier saints went through, like laceration by a wheel of swords (George), pierced with arrows (Sebastian), etc. I am absolutely opposed to torture, but I find the context interesting, including who does it and for what reasons. Rome used torture to get Christians to deny their faith, and the United States of America (called a "Christian nation" by some) uses it to extract information.
3. *Catechism*, paragraph 1776.
4. Camilo's self-description of his relationship with the Roman Catholic Church, shared with me in a conversation during our tenure on the board of advisors for Brite Divinity School's Soul Repair Center, http://www.britesoulrepair.org.

Nate Wildermuth

1979–present

For many on active duty, the terrorist attacks on September 11, 2001, had a galvanizing effect. Our national pride and identity were solidified and we felt very much at one with America in opposing this new and grave threat that had showed itself. But for at least one soldier, 9/11 had the opposite effect.

A desire to be the best drove young Nate Wildermuth to pursue the hardest, most grueling path in the military he could find. Enlisting at age twenty, he signed up for airborne training and from there went on to volunteer for the elite Ranger Battalions, under the Joint Special Operations Command with Special Forces and Navy SEALs. As a forward observer for the artillery in this prestigious unit, he had enormous destructive capabilities. After less than a year in a Ranger unit, he decided he could do better, and sought an endorsement from his commanding officer to be admitted into the United States Military Academy at West Point. In July 2001, he got his wish, and he shipped off for New York state. There, he joined the highly selective skydiving team and quickly rose to fourth in his class.

But throughout all his accomplishments, he describes how there was something going on within him, something nobody could see from the

outside. When the towers were hit months later, and his class watched televised reports of ash billowing in the sky above the Pentagon, his classmates all got fired up to go to war. Nate, however, was struck even more decisively by a need for profound reflection. As his country raced to war, he stopped to ponder what was really happening.[1]

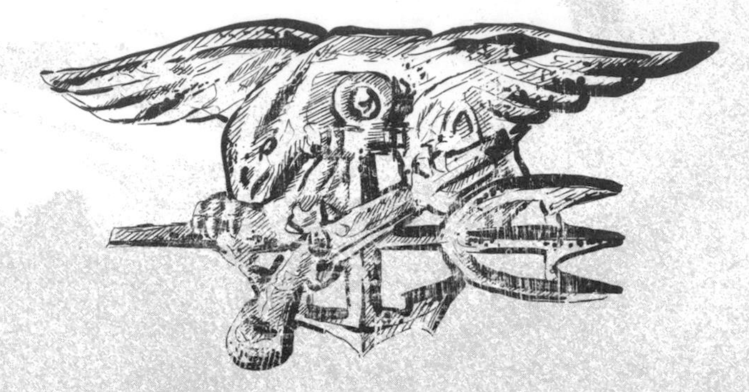

A Roman Catholic, he attended daily mass at West Point and was there when the archbishop for the military services, Cardinal Edwin Frederick O'Brien, delivered a homily suggesting that Pope John Paul II's condemnation of the wars was not from his seat of authority[2] and therefore was not binding on Catholics in the military. By then, he had read Leo Tolstoy's *The Kingdom of God Is Within You* and had strong feelings of pacifism that were only strengthened when he heard the cardinal's rather unorthodox refutation of the pope.

After seeing "shock and awe" in Iraq and hearing from Cardinal O'Brien, Nate applied in 2003 to be a conscientious objector and be discharged from his contractual obligations to the Army. He had an easier time than most applicants, who often face severe stigma within their units as being cowardly or derelict in their duties. Centurions Guild frequently hears from service members who are verbally attacked for requesting CO status, as Desmond Doss was in his medical

1. Nate began writing an autobiography, which you can preview at http://www.kickstarter.com/projects/285752/so-youre-a-coward-a-memoir-of-conscientious-object.
2. This concept is called *ex cathedra*, a Latin phrase meaning "from the chair," otherwise referred to by Protestants (somewhat inaccurately) as meaning papal infallibility. *Ex cathedra* has been invoked only twice in the history of the Roman Catholic Church, each time concerning doctrines about Mary, Jesus' mother.

unit before he went to Iwo Jima and eventually earned his Medal of Honor.[3] Nate's investigating officer was also Catholic, and remarked that he agreed with Nate. Like a number of cadets whose conscience is crystallized, Nate faced the threat of having to pay back the money the government put into his education. In Nate's case, because he was put on a leave of absence pending his conscientious objector application, he was accused of "willfully failing" his classes and charged $100,000. He won on appeal by one vote and was discharged peacefully by December 2003.

Once out, he went to live in a Catholic Worker community near his family in Washington, D.C. The Catholic Worker movement began in 1929, growing out of the visions of Dorothy Day and Peter Maurin to create places in which Christian works of mercy were performed: feeding the hungry, giving drink to the thirsty, clothing the naked, sheltering the homeless, caring for the sick, and visiting the imprisoned.[4]

★ ★ ★

Nate lived beside people deprived of homes and health care by the new wars, people he had never taken the time to come to know before. At the Catholic Worker community his crystallization of conscience really solidified and he expressed his pacifism.[5] Nate's life is one example of many of steadfast courage and determination, guiding us all to live in right relationship with our neighbors, which he did with his fellow cadets and, later, with strangers suffering and in need.

3. See page 154 for more on Desmond T. Doss, the first conscientious objector to be awarded his nation's highest award for valor in combat.
4. The Catholic Worker movement is by its nature decentralized. However, some useful information is online at http://www.catholicworker.org. The Corporeal Works of Mercy are based on Matthew 25:34-40, within the parable of the sheep and the goats.
5. While living there he also received a call from a young fellow forward observer from Hawaii—yours truly—whose own convictions were in flux.

Zach grew up in a devout Christian family, watched Fox News, and read the Scriptures front to back. It was only natural that Zach felt a connection with the centurion from the book of Acts.[1] After all, he shared his name. Like Cornelius, he wanted to be a military commander. So at eighteen, when he got into college, he joined the Air Force Reserve Officer Training Corps (AFROTC). Upon graduation, he could look forward to being commissioned as a second lieutenant in the Air Force.

He excelled in school, receiving the Gold Award for ranking second among all his peers, and by the end of his sophomore year, he was awarded the Silver for being at the top of his class. He was following the path of the first Christian Gentile, centurion Cornelius, in being a God-fearing person of authority. Zach led the Officer Christian Fellowship in his detachment, conducting weekly Bible studies, thinking that by connecting his Christian faith to military leadership he would ensure that God would favor him as God did Saint Cornelius.

But then his life was ruined.

---

1. See page 48 for more on Saint Cornelius, the first Gentile baptized into the church.

While painting murals[2] and passing out Christmas presents to poor families during a visit to Philadelphia, the City of Brotherly Love, Zach met many Christians whose lives hinted at a renunciation of war and violence. He was supposed to be graduating from his program and completing the requirements for joining the Air Force in eight months. Now, after nearly two years of questions, readings, prayers, and personal conversations, he told his detachment commander that the kingdom of God is here, that he felt overwhelmingly convinced that he should no longer study or prepare for war.[3] It didn't go over well; applying for conscientious objector status is never popular, especially with two wars raging. His commander was a colonel recently returning from the war effort in Afghanistan. "I just got back from the war," he told Zach. "I am a Christian and have been since I was eight. I have worn this uniform for twenty-one years, so tell me why the Christian faith I hold is incompatible with military service?"

With a little fear in his heart and trembling in his bones, Zach proceeded to explain to his superior that he could no longer train to be a officer. Eventually he

2. Zach appears in Shane Claiborne's book, *The Irresistible Revolution* (Grand Rapids, MI: Zondervan, 2006), on page 141 as the veteran who joins the Simple Way for a time to paint murals, but at the time requested to remain anonymous.
3. Isaiah 2:4 and Micah 4:3.

was granted status as a conscientious objector and released from his contract. Like Nate Wildermuth before him, he had to pay back some tuition, but it was a small price to pay for the ease of his conscience.

Like Cornelius before him, Zach experienced conversion, his convictions putting him at odds with the world's reigning superpower. Just after applying for conscientious objection, he and some friends moved into a small neighborhood on the west side of Cincinnati. They experienced firsthand the violence the area was known for: one roommate was pistol-whipped; another was robbed at gunpoint in front of their house. A friend, Chris, who was homeless with no legs below his knees, lived with them for six months but was killed by gunfire. Ironically, after separating from the military to live more peaceably, Zach found himself immersed in more violence. But he recognized that he wasn't the first to experience this paradox. Oscar Romero's words inspired him during that beautifully difficult time:

> We have never preached violence, except the violence of love, which left Christ nailed to a cross, the violence that we must each do to ourselves to overcome our selfishness and such cruel inequalities among us. The violence we preach is not the violence of the sword, the violence of hatred. It is the violence of love, of brotherhood, the violence that wills to beat weapons into plowshares.[4]

Today, Zach is the cofounder of Centurions Guild, a small group of service members and veterans who are committed to serving fellow Christian soldiers in discerning the line between God and country. For more information, see www.centurionsguild.org. ☧

4. Oscar Romero, *The Violence of Love* (Rifton, NY: Plough, 2011), 25. From an entry dated November 27, 1977.

Appendixes

Appendix 1

A Few More Mischief Makers: Howard Zinn, Philip Berrigan, and David Cortright

Military service is very good at instilling order and respect in those who partake in it. Good soldiers are thought to be obedient soldiers, men and women who strictly observe the laws of the land. But the problem with rules is that they must be broken when they do not bend toward justice, with what Martin Luther King Jr. called "the long arc of the moral universe." So every now and then peculiar kinds of soldiers march to the beat of a slightly different drummer. These folks are known for the hell they raise, but it's usually to force hell out of hiding.

★ ★ ★

Howard Zinn was a rabble-rouser known for his People's History series of books. He took the field of history and turned it on its head. Where before the victors were assumed to have written history, he insisted that the oppressed and the conquered had just as much to say, if not more, about how we should view our own social evolution. History is deeply political, he would say.

Born into a Jewish immigrant family in Brooklyn, New York, Howard read voraciously as a child. When World War II broke out, he was eager to fight fascism and Nazism in Europe, so he entered the Air

Force and became a bomber pilot. His experience dropping bombs and reading altered "official reports" led him to question the reliability of established historical methods. When Zinn came home, he attended New York University on the GI Bill, moving on quickly to an MA and PhD at Columbia. As a historian, he insisted that the official story was not always the only story, and sometimes not even a factual story. Against a pessimistic view that the status quo was written in stone upon the hearts of human civilization, he said, "I don't believe in [pessimism]. It's not simply a matter of faith, but of historical evidence. Not overwhelming evidence, just enough to give hope, because for hope we don't need certainty, only possibility."[1]

★ ★ ★

Philip Berrigan. As Catholic priests during the war in Vietnam, Philip and Daniel Berrigan were famous for their antiwar stance. They vehemently opposed the conflict, burning draft cards, leading nonviolent movements, and being imprisoned a number of times for actions aimed at criticizing the American war effort. They even spent some time on the FBI's top ten most wanted list.

Before his life of protest, however, Philip was drafted into the artillery during the Second World War at just twenty years of age. He went through boot camp at Camp Gordon, Georgia, and saw racism in its most raw and distilled form, seeing blacks "seventy-five years after their emancipation from slavery . . . living in brutal poverty, kept down by Jim Crow laws and racist violence."[2] He sailed to Europe on the famous *Queen Mary* in the dead of winter, with the white soldiers sleeping in heated berths on bunk beds, never seeming to care when they passed their black brothers huddled together on deck in nothing but blankets and stocking caps. Within two years, he participated in the Battle of the Bulge in Europe and was commissioned as an officer

1. From a speech he gave in 1990, featured on the Zinn Education Project website, http://www.zinnedproject.org, accessed June 3, 2013.
2. Philip Berrigan, *Fighting the Lamb's War*, (Munroe, ME: Common Courage Press, 1996), 15–16.

for his service. He crossed branches and entered the infantry.

Philip's experience in war led him to have a very stark perspective on issues of justice and peace, particularly American racism and nuclear armament. He entered an order of Josephite priests, whose work focused on solidarity with African Americans. As a priest, he joined his brother Daniel in protest after protest, especially those that highlighted the proliferation of nuclear weapons and humankind's newfound ability to destroy the entire world God had created. He felt his years as an antiwar activist were a form of penance, atoning for the things he witnessed and was a part of as an American soldier.[3] He was a part of the group that founded the Plowshares Movement.

★ ★ ★

David Cortright is a Gandhi scholar and a preeminent authority on peace movements. He has written a number of books on sanctions and incentives in international conflict and their effect on peacemaking. He has testified before Congress a number of times and has spent time serving the United States Institute of Peace. He currently teaches at the University of Notre Dame, at the Kroc Institute of International Peace Studies. His interests in peace emerged directly from his own experience of war. From 1969 to 1971, he went back and forth between graduate studies in Indiana and military service in Vietnam, eventually coming to oppose war and seek viable alternatives to war fighting. His first book, *Soldiers in Revolt: The American Military Today*, was a groundbreaking study of dissent within the ranks of the US military, published the same year he completed his PhD. ☧

3. I wish I could have found a profile to help incorporate the use of penitential rites for knights and crusaders returning from war in the medieval period. Having ceremonial returns for veterans is something that I find promising, and I would direct anyone else with interest to Bernard J. Verkamp, *Moral Treatment of Returning Warriors in Early Medieval and Modern Times* (Scranton, PA: University of Scranton Press, 2006). A more contemporary resource for modern churches would be D.A. Thompson and D. Wetterstrom, *Beyond the Yellow Ribbon: Ministering to Returning Combat Veterans* (Nashville, TN: Abingdon Press, 2009).

Appendix 2

Creeds

Before the invention of printing presses, LED projectors, and sound technicians, memorization was the primary learning tool for a largely illiterate and persecuted community of believers. Christians recited creeds, the church's earliest statements of faith, as a means to remember the faith that they adhered to, but also to affirm and proclaim their trust and love for their Commander in Chief when they were outed for their faith.

The first creed was the Apostles' Creed, which varied slightly across different churches in Rome and the ancient Near East, because the persecutions made communication dangerous and unreliable. After the state no longer persecuted the church, Christians held a major council in a city called Nicaea. For the first time the different Christian communities could communicate openly and begin to settle theological variations that had arisen from their isolation from each other. The Nicene Creed is more specific in its language and survives to this day as a formidable statement of faith for many Christian traditions. The following is an excerpt from the first half of the creed:

> We believe in one God,
> the Father, the Almighty,
> maker of heaven and earth,
> of all that is, seen and unseen.
>
> We believe in one Lord, Jesus Christ,
> the only Son of God,
> eternally begotten of the Father,
> God from God, Light from Light,

true God from true God,
begotten, not made,
of one Being with the Father.
Through him all things were made.
For us and for our salvation
he came down from heaven:
by the power of the Holy Spirit
he became incarnate from the Virgin Mary,
and was made man . . . [1]

Many militaries have their own creeds too. The US military uses the term *creed* for "an oath or saying that provides a value structure by which to live or work. Creeds then set the tone of life."[2] Notice that military creeds do not require common beliefs or intellectual assent—just actions. In other words, you can live (and die) by military creeds and oaths without fully believing the thing to which you swear. But Christian creeds and vows (like those taken at our baptism) expect that we believe in our hearts as well, that we have faith not just in our words and deeds.

Creeds of the various branches of the US military emphasize the values particular to them:[3]

- The mission of an airman is "to fly, fight, and win."
- Soldiers swear to "deploy, engage, and destroy the enemies of the United States of America in close combat."
- Sailors "represent the fighting spirit of the Navy and those who have gone before" them.
- The Marines vow, in their Rifleman's Creed, that their rifle is their best friend and their life. "Before God," they swear, their

1. The Nicene Creed is available at various Internet sites and in denominational worship books. The translation I lean toward is from the *Book of Common Prayer* that the Episcopal Church in America uses. See http://www.episcopalchurch.org/page/creeds.
2. Quote from http://www.military.com/join-armed-forces/military-creeds.html, retrieved June 3, 2013.
3. A good point of reference, again, is http://www.military.com/join-armed-forces/military-creeds.html.

> rifle and themselves "are the masters of our enemy. We are the saviors of my life."

Where do such statements leave God? In Isaiah, the people of God are warned against trusting in the strength of their weapons and the skill of their warriors.[4] Instead, we are to trust in God for our well-being. In fact, survival is not a virtue; Christians must acknowledge that God's will for our lives might lead to our physical demise, but it is also the first step toward our resurrection, for in the Nicene Creed, "we look forward to the resurrection of the dead, and the life of the world to come."[5]

"Survival is not a virtue; Christians must acknowledge that God's will for our lives might lead to our physical demise, but it is also the first step toward our resurrection."

That is what we Christians say we believe when we recite the creed. The deep irony is that people are often ready to die in the military without necessarily believing in what they are doing, while as Christians we can state what we believe without necessarily being ready to die for our faith. On the one hand, the church could learn from the military what it means to be prepared to actually give our lives to something, while the military could learn from the church what it means to be a people of conscientious engagement in what they know is a fallible, even corrupt institution.[6] ☧

---

4. Isaiah 31:1-3.
5. http://www.episcopalchurch.org/page/creeds.
6. I would argue that the visible, militant church is corrupt insofar as it is human and exists prior to the final coming of Christ. Call it original sin if it fits, but as a church under grace prior to the eschaton, I hope it is not a totally foreign idea that, even on its best days, it is still corrupt. On the other hand, for the military, the culture that prevailed in my six years was such that, while we might make jokes, we never sincerely believed the government system itself was fundamentally flawed. The church and the military, being human institutions, are each corrupt. The former, however, being simultaneously divine (as the body of Christ) will not ultimately perish, while the latter most certainly will.

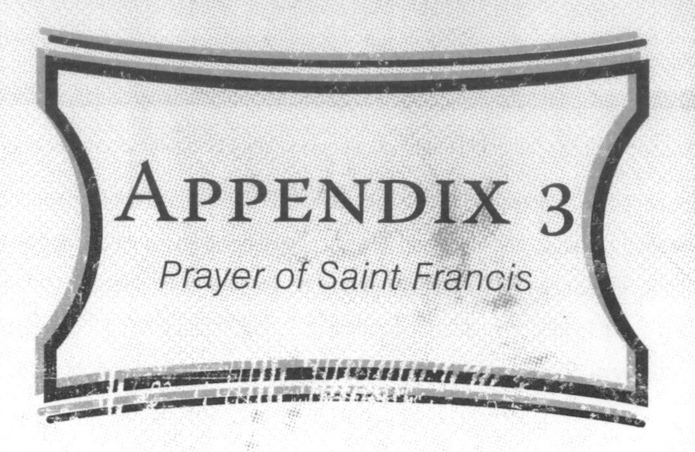

Appendix 3

Prayer of Saint Francis

The Prayer of Saint Francis is a popular prayer among soldiers and chaplains. Sometimes it can be seen scribbled on the insides of Kevlar helmets or shoved in muddied cargo pockets. Francis himself was a soldier saint who turned his back on war in 1204, when many Western, Roman Catholic Christians went to Constantinople on a Crusade to sack the capital and its Christians, now belonging to the Eastern (Orthodox) Church. It was not the church's finest hour, and we may thank God for sparing young Francis that horror.

But the prayer attributed to him does not trace its origin to the thirteenth century, when Francis lived. There are varying stories on how it came to be. Edward Tick, a noted veteran psychologist and author of *War and the Soul,*[1] has claimed that it originated in World War I, when a chaplain found the prayer scrawled on the back of a Saint Francis prayer card and left in an empty helmet in the trenches. The first time the prayer appeared in publication was in December 1912, in the French Christian magazine *La Clochette,* or "The Little Bell." Tick recites it periodically at retreats he hosts for veterans and civilians organized for the healing of hidden war wounds such as PTSD and moral injury.[2]

---

1. Edward Tick, *War and the Soul: Healing Our Nation's Veterans from Post-Traumatic Stress Disorder* (Wheaton, IL: Quest, 2005).
2. Tick's organization, Soldier's Heart (www.soldiersheart.net), hosts multiple retreats every year for soldiers and civilians alike. While I have not attended one myself, a few close friends have done so and recommended them highly.

We might never know for sure how the prayer came to be in its final form. And yet soldiers and veterans alike find encouragement in it:

> Lord, make me an instrument of your peace.
> Where there is hatred, let me sow love.
> Where there is injury, pardon.
> Where there is doubt, faith.
> Where there is despair, hope.
> Where there is darkness, light.
> Where there is sadness, joy.
> O Divine Master,
> grant that I may not so much seek to be consoled, as to console;
> to be understood, as to understand;
> to be loved, as to love.
> For it is in giving that we receive.
> It is in pardoning that we are pardoned,
> and it is in dying that we are born to Eternal Life.
> Amen.

APPENDIX 4

Chaplains

In 2012, Milites Christi, a student group at Duke University Divinity School, led a panel discussion titled "What Is a Chaplain?" The student group was formed in order to cultivate conversations about war, faith, and soldiering, so the Latin phrase for "soldiers of Christ" seemed appropriate. Our weapons are prayer, our armor is faith, and our commander is Jesus.[1] But chaplains are also in prisons, hospitals, and even in organizations like Veterans for Peace.

So what is a chaplain? In order to understand what chaplains are, it helps to know their historical origins. Chaplains date back to the fourth-century church in France. They were the monks in charge of guarding the relics of Saint Martin of Tours, including his cape, or in Latin, *capella* (literally "little cape"). Those trusted to guard it came to be called *capellani*, which, when Latin was replaced by French, evolved into *chapelein*—chaplain. Because of the fame of the relics, they had to be housed in a protected room adjacent to the church they called home, which in French became *chapelle*—the origin of "chapel."

Martin's cape might provide some figurative ground to understand modern chaplains today. The beautiful cloak represented his assignment to a prestigious military unit, a kind of border between church and state. When he split his cape to clothe a freezing beggar, Martin

1. Unfortunately, no one preserved records of the panel, but you can learn more about Milites Christi's work with veterans in the church at http://sites.duke.edu/aftertheyellowribbon/schedule.

was guarding this boundary. Chaplains to this day share in this heritage; they guard the line between God and country, making sure that one does not bleed into the other inappropriately. When necessary, they pull the two apart long enough to see when and where one ends and the other begins. Ultimately, the job of chaplains is to serve God and country (in that order).

"Chaplain" is a position, a title usually assigned by the state, for the military, prisons, state-run hospitals, and other agencies. The title given by the church for that vocation is "pastor," "father," or "reverend." While they may have chapels—smaller rooms that serve specific functions—churches do not have chaplains.

Military chaplaincy is particularly interesting because of its proximity to state violence and the diversity of theologies around war and peace. Different people therefore understand chaplaincy differently. George Zabelka felt that "as a Catholic priest my task was to keep my people, wherever they were, close to the mind and heart of Christ. As a military chaplain I was to try to see that the boys conducted themselves according to the teachings of the Catholic Church and Christ on war. . . . I often had to enter the world of the boys who were losing their minds because of something they did in war."[2] Francis Sampson, however, believed that "Priests and soldiers are both called to identical things—that is—the preservation of peace, the establishment of justice when it has been lost, and the providing of security with protection for the weak and the innocent."[3] These are not necessarily opposing perspectives, but Zabelka and Sampson, while both fighting in World War II, responded differently to the state-sanctioned violence that they observed firsthand.

Chaplains' jobs in the military are also defined by regulations that expect them to be both religious leaders and command advisors. All

2. Quoted in Charles C. McCarthy's "A-Bomb Chaplain Regrets 'Utter Moral Corruption' of Civilian Mass Killing," *Catholic San Francisco*, August 9, 2011.
3. From www.missioncapodanno.org.

chaplains are expected to deploy in war settings, but they will not carry a weapon. Eight chaplains have won the US Congressional Medal of Honor:

1. **John M. Whitehead**—Protestant Civil War chaplain who carried wounded to safety and administered care under fire at Stones River, Tennessee, in 1862.
2. **Francis B. Hall**—Very similar activity at Salem Heights, Virginia, in 1863.
3. **Milton Lorenzi Haney**—Third Civil War chaplain in 1864, unique in having forfeited his noncombatant status by carrying a musket.
4. **Joseph T. O'Callahan**—Jesuit Navy chaplain in World War II who heroically aided the wounded and administered care aboard the sinking *USS Franklin* in 1945, which had come within one hundred miles of the Japanese mainland.
5. **Emil Joseph Kapaun**—First service period during World War II in Burma, discharged and reentered a few years later to get shipped to Korea, where he was captured in November, 1950. Spent seven months ministering to fellow prisoners of war and stealing food, medicine, and communication equipment for them before he died on May 23, 1951. The Vatican is considering making Father Emil a saint in the Roman Catholic Church.
6. **Charles Joseph Watters**—Upon an ambush in Dak To, Vietnam, in 1967, he rushed to the point of contact in order to administer last rites and courageously aid the wounded. Soon after, he was killed by friendly fire.

7. **Vincent Robert Cappodanno**—Navy chaplain serving in Quang Tin Province, Vietnam, in 1967 when his unit came under heavy fire. Aided Marine corpsmen (medic) while also providing spiritual care after having his hand partially severed by mortar fire. Killed in action as he tried to save a wounded corpsman. Father Vincent is also being considered for sainthood in the Roman Catholic Church.
8. **Angelo (Charles) Liteky**—In Vietnam in 1967, sprang to the assistance of two wounded soldiers when his unit was defending against an ambush in Bien Hoa Province. Wounded in the leg and neck while taking twenty men to the safety of a nearby landing zone. Disenfranchised with the military after the war, however, he became the first awardee to return his Medal of Honor, to President Ronald Reagan, in 1986.

Appendix 5

Firefighters

More than a few times, I have been asked in what service occupations Christians might be employed if the violence of the military or police forces conflict with their convictions. The military, after all, is designed to defend democracy and freedom and the police enforce justice and protect the innocent. Are there no uniformed services that don't employ violence, so that Christians can engage in national or community service without being expected to be ready to kill?

My answer is always pretty direct: become a firefighter. Firefighters do not carry firearms (yet) and spend their non-fire-related time accompanying ambulances on 911 calls, helping kittens out of trees, and keeping in peak physical condition. But it hasn't always been so rosy. Fire companies used to be privately operated, and would compete against other companies and engines to put out fires—services for which they would then charge massive sums. Eventually, firefighting was absorbed under local governments and the costs were defrayed by taxpayer money, a reflection of the common commitment of the entire community in ensuring that every house be safe from the dangers of fire.

But firefighting has an older history. An ancient Roman governor, Crassus, was the first to collect men to fight fires, but he did so quite shrewdly. At the first cry of alarm, his men would race to the scene, and then wait while Crassus negotiated a price with the (probably irate) property owner. If it burned, Crassus would buy it at a pittance, thus acquiring great fortune at the direct expense of others in need.

By the first century, the caesar decided he would improve the system by employing slaves to avoid the debacle of the privately operated system begun by Crassus. Eventually, the fire brigades were governed by the military system and were called the *Vigiles*, for they kept vigil over the city of Rome, not just against fires, but also against burglars and runaway slaves.

By the third century, these units were made part of the Praetorian prefects, reporting directly to Caesar. A man called Florian (see story on page 78), who always carried with him a pitcher of water, commanded one such unit. Florian was exposed as a secret Christian in 303, under the reign of Diocletian, and was ironically drowned in a river, from which he would draw water to help save Roman homes and lives in the event of fires. To this day, Florian is the patron saint of firefighters, and his cross is used widely for firefighting companies.

The Lord's Prayer petitions God to "forgive us our debts, *as we also have forgiven* our debtors."[1] We ask God for the same forgiveness that we ourselves distribute. We will be generous in our mercy so that we may experience God's mercy to us. Francis's prayer sums it up beautifully with the words "It is in pardoning that we are pardoned."

A related word, sometimes used synonymously with *forgiveness,* is *amnesty*. Coming home from Iraq, we were allowed to use "amnesty boxes" while in transit through Kuwait. Any contraband could be dropped into these red boxes without any questions asked, anything from live ammo to war trophies—anything that was otherwise forbidden from being removed from whatever country we had been deployed to. Back home in our communities, sometimes police departments host amnesty days, where anyone can bring in unregistered weapons or other illegal material without being charged. Amnesty is what the Truth and Reconciliation Commission in South Africa fostered and cultivated. Enemies faced one another and pardoned one another for past sins, in exchange for the truth.

One major act of amnesty of the last half century in the United States was toward those who refused to fight in Vietnam. This war was highly

1. Matthew 6:12. Also, Luke 11:4.

contentious, leaving communities and churches divided over the justifiability of the conflict. Many conscientious Christian men faced the draft without being given the option of nonviolent service. Tragically, few churches were a part of the sanctuary movement, which provided protection for these recruits when they became convinced of the war's moral inadequacies.[2] Some of them fled to Canada to keep from violating their consciences. If they were drafted and did not show up, they became felons, fugitives from the law for refusing to acquiesce to moral compromise. They were called "draft dodgers."

Draft dodgers have John Vianney of Ars as their patron saint. Just as John received amnesty from Napoleon in 1810, they too got their shot at freedom. Their pardoner was not a French emperor, but a Baptist Sunday school teacher from Georgia and the thirty-ninth president of the United States of America, Jimmy Carter. On January 21, 1977 (one day after his inauguration), Carter officially granted amnesty to all Vietnam War resistors who fled their homes in pursuit of moral or theological integrity. Many came home to cold receptions, if they came home at all. They might be soldiers of a different stripe, marching to a different drummer, but theirs was a fight nonetheless, born of deep convictions that prohibited them from participating in a war they or their church found to be unjust.

2. I have heard of a few scattered churches who protected draft evaders and soldiers (then called "GIs") who felt the Vietnam War did not qualify as a just war (see appendix 8). One church of note is the Church of the Crossroads in Honolulu, Hawaii, where over thirty such men were kept safe for over one month before military police stormed the building in which they were being fed (nutritionally and spiritually). Read more in *The Crossroads Witness*, by Betty and Robert Hemphill (University of Hawaii, 1988), a rare but important book, available if you contact church administrators: http://churchofthecrossroadshawaii.org.

Appendix 7

Hymns

Music had a concrete effect on my ongoing recovery from the hidden wounds of war that I acquired in Iraq in 2004.[1] Music remains integral to this day to me and a number of other veterans.[2] The reason for this is that music can say things in pace, tone, and volume that mere words often do not accomplish. After all, who belts out the Apostles' or Rifleman's Creed in the shower, holding a bar of soap as though it's a microphone? Singing is something unique and distinct from the spoken word, even though perhaps we can think of examples that challenge that sharp distinction (such as slam poetry, which many vets I know have taken up).

For Christians, music is related to some of the oldest Scriptures that we know. According to some biblical scholars, the song of Deborah[3] is one of the oldest parts of the Bible, one of the first things to be included in the Hebrew canon.[4] It is a victory hymn, so we see that war and song are tightly bound together, sometimes difficult to pull apart.

---

1. I talk about music in my introduction and scattered throughout *Reborn on the Fourth of July* (Downers Grove, IL: InterVarsity Press, 2012).
2. The work of Jason Moon comes to mind specifically. See the work he has done leveraging music for veterans' healing with an organization he began, Warrior Songs, Inc.—http://www.warriorsongs.org. He also has an album of work that covers his own movement from soldier to veteran: *Trying to Find My Way Home* (Pewaukee, WI: Full Moon Music, 2010).
3. Judges 5:2-31. Also, see page 23 for my reflection on the story of Deborah and Jael.
4. Who knew I would remember something from my Old Testament survey course in seminary? This comes from Michael D. Coogan, *A Brief Introduction to the Old Testament: The Hebrew Bible in Its Context* (London, UK: Oxford, 2009), 180.

Similarly, after crossing the Red Sea in Exodus 15, the songs of Moses and Miriam celebrate their escape from the all-powerful Egyptian military. But oral tradition records ancient Jewish commentary[5] suggesting God took satisfaction neither in destroying his creation and the Egyptian charioteers and horsemen nor in seeing the Israelites jumping for joy at the demise of God's enemies. Songs of celebration are not always the best response to our violence, though they sometimes get the most attention.[6]

Music, like creeds, aided the early church in the education of new converts (who were largely illiterate) by giving more ways in which to memorize the faith they were entering. In the church, we sing hymns to this day; they contain theological significance and help reinforce the message from the pulpit. So, too, in expressions of patriotism: people sing their national anthem, often using physical or symbolic gestures of loyalty. In the United States, many people will put their hand over their hearts. In the military, we call cadences while we exercise in the mornings and hear taps as the twilight comes in the evening. Music gives shape to our lives whether we notice it or not.

Whether in our hymns or national anthems, we should take care in what we sing, no matter how inconsequential it might seem. After all, Jesus reminds us in the gospel of Matthew, things that come *out* of our mouths can either defile or sanctify us, not so much things that go in.[7]

I have noticed over the years that some denominational hymnals include national anthems like "America the Beautiful" or the "Star-Spangled Banner." Conversely, in the United States—a land that claims to maintain a separation between church and state—I notice people using Christian hymns in national ceremonies. The line

5. This particular reflection comes from the Babylonian Talmud, Megillah 10b, which reads "At that time [of the exodus] the ministering angels wanted to chant their hymns before the Holy One, blessed be God, but God said, 'The work of my hands is being drowned in the sea, and shall you chant hymns before me?'"
6. Again, I commend to you the work of Jason Moon, especially his songs "Trying to Find My Way Home" and "Hold On."
7. Matthew 15. See also appendix 2, on creeds.

between religious and patriotic songs can be difficult to navigate, and it may not be easy to discern whether or not it successfully separates state and church—or how much we even want it to. A few songs in particular tease out how our loyalties pan out and can help us see the line between God and country with more stark clarity. The following are especially worthy of note.

Onward Christian Soldiers (Sabine Baring-Gould, 1865)

Sabine Baring-Gould originally wrote this hymn for British schoolchildren. Baring-Gould used a number of allusions to 2 Timothy 2:3, in which the apostle Paul writes to his friend about being a soldier of Christ, as well as a few other references to the church being like an army. As I discovered, this is not uncommon in church history, given the early church's habit of subverting imperial language to service for God instead.

It is unclear exactly when the hymn became popular outside Britain, though as early as 1941, it was sung during an international service on the naval vessel *H.M.S. Prince of Wales*, where Prime Minister Winston Churchill was meeting with President Franklin Roosevelt. Churchill chose it, as well as the rest of the hymns sung for that service, because he believed that God had ordained the Second World War to overcome Nazi aggression in Europe: "Here was the only hope, but also the sure hope, of saving the world from measureless degradation."[8] Troublingly, he overlooked God as our hope and Christ as our Savior from degradation. The song caught on in America, later being sung at the funeral for Dwight Eisenhower in the National Cathedral, but in the same years also being used by the burgeoning civil rights movement that often ran in opposition to many of the national policies and trends. The lyrics are as follows:

8. Ace Collins, *Stories Behind the Hymns That Inspire America* (Grand Rapids, MI: Zondervan, 2003), 153–154.

Onward, Christian soldiers, marching as to war,
with the cross of Jesus going on before.
Christ, the royal Master, leads against the foe;
forward into battle see his banners go!

Refrain:
Onward, Christian soldiers, marching as to war,
with the cross of Jesus going on before.

At the sign of triumph Satan's host doth flee;
on then, Christian soldiers, on to victory!
Hell's foundations quiver at the shout of praise;
brothers, lift your voices, loud your anthems raise.

(Refrain)

Like a mighty army moves the church of God;
brothers, we are treading where the saints have trod.
We are not divided, all one body we,
one in hope and doctrine, one in charity.

(Refrain)

Crowns and thrones may perish, kingdoms rise and wane,
but the church of Jesus constant will remain.
Gates of hell can never 'gainst that church prevail;
we have Christ's own promise, and that cannot fail.

(Refrain)

Onward then, ye people, join our happy throng,
blend with ours your voices in the triumph song.
Glory, laud, and honor unto Christ the King,
this through countless ages men and angels sing.

(Refrain)

"The New Testament's use of war as a metaphor is not a rallying cry for the craftiness of a serpent, but an altar call for the innocence of a dove."

What is being done theologically in this song? It sounds much like Moses's song from Exodus, and indeed people and angels may sing this way, but at what cost? There is a place for celebration and God is without question deserving of praise, but the context should be given much more credence. Christians do not celebrate the necessity of violence, but mourn that it must occur. War is no topic for excitement. The New Testament's use of war as a metaphor is not a rallying cry for the craftiness of a serpent, but an altar call for the innocence of a dove, "For our struggle is not against enemies of blood and flesh, but against the rulers, against the authorities, against the cosmic powers of this present darkness, against the spiritual forces of evil."[9] To incorporate Scripture into our musical worship is time-tested and healthy, but our choice of texts and our interpretation thereof is critical to the life and integrity of the church. Compare "Onward Christian Soldiers," then, to another song that sings of God and strength of arms.

Mary's Magnificat[10]

My soul magnifies the Lord,
and my spirit rejoices in God my Savior,
for he has looked with favor on the lowliness of his servant.
    Surely, from now on all generations will call me blessed;
for the Mighty One has done great things for me,
    and holy is his name.

9. Ephesians 6:12, New Revised Standard Version. *Powers* is the same Greek word (*exousia*) that Paul uses for earthly entities in Romans 13:1. *Authorities* and *rulers* are frequently also used in other translations of the Romans passage. Notice, however, that Paul is not making a sweeping claim about all (spiritual or earthly) authority; the fact that he seems to be saying opposite things in Romans (be subject to) and Ephesians (struggle against) should clue us in to the fact that there is nuance to his theology.
10. Luke 1:46-55 NRSV.

His mercy is for those who fear him
    from generation to generation.
He has shown strength with his arm;
    he has scattered the proud in the thoughts of their hearts.
He has brought down the powerful from their thrones,
    and lifted up the lowly;
he has filled the hungry with good things,
    and sent the rich away empty.
He has helped his servant Israel,
    in remembrance of his mercy,
according to the promise he made to our ancestors,
    to Abraham and to his descendants forever.

Mary is not concerned here with *whether* crowns and thrones may perish or kingdoms wane, but that God has already done so. To propose lyrically, as Baring-Gould does, that the church is still marching as if to war is to overlook that the war has been won already by the victory of the cross. Furthermore, Mary speaks as someone from below the status quo, and she rejoices that the status of the proud, the powerful, and the rich *has been* reversed by the God of mercy, who favors the lowly.

Battle Hymn of the Republic (Julia Ward Howe, 1861)

Here we have another woman, like Mary, who writes in literal proximity to her children. While Mary rejoiced that she was given a son who was to be the Christ, Howe wrote her hymn late one night near her sleeping children. Julia was later to witness the American Civil War, where sometimes even brothers, or fathers and sons, fought against one another on opposite sides and family values were shaken. But now she wrote the hymn as a rallying cry for the Northern states, which were fighting against slavery and the Southern states' right to secede from the Union that the original colonies formed after the Revolutionary War.

Mine eyes have seen the glory of the coming of the Lord:[11]
He is trampling out the vintage where the grapes of wrath are stored;
He hath loosed the fateful lightning of His terrible swift sword:
His truth is marching on.

Chorus:
Glory, glory, hallelujah!
Glory, glory, hallelujah!
Glory, glory, hallelujah!
His truth is marching on.

I have seen Him in the watch-fires of a hundred circling camps,
They have builded Him an altar in the evening dews and damps;
I can read His righteous sentence by the dim and flaring lamps:
His day is marching on.

(Chorus)

I have read a fiery gospel writ in burnished rows of steel:
"As ye deal with my contemners, so with you my grace shall deal;
Let the Hero, born of woman, crush the serpent with his heel,
Since God is marching on."

(Chorus)

He has sounded forth the trumpet that shall never call retreat;
He is sifting out the hearts of men before His judgment-seat:
Oh, be swift, my soul, to answer Him! be jubilant, my feet!
Our God is marching on.

11. The "glory of the coming of the Lord" was seen by Simeon and Anna in Luke 2, at Jesus' presentation at the temple as a baby.

(Chorus)

In the beauty of the lilies Christ was born across the sea,
With a glory in His bosom that transfigures you and me:
As He died to make men holy, let us die to make men free,
While God is marching on.

(Chorus)

He is coming like the glory of the morning on the wave,
He is Wisdom to the mighty, He is Succour to the brave,
So the world shall be His footstool, and the soul of Time His slave,
Our God is marching on.

(Chorus)

The song became hugely popular across the Northern states during the Civil War, which turned out to be the bloodiest in American history. It finally ended, but not before it claimed the lives of over six hundred thousand fathers, brothers, and sons. Perhaps only then could Howe see as Mary saw, that indeed God had scattered and brought down many things, including her faith in war and the idealism that violence can be spoken of so glowingly. As I mention in her profile,[12] it was not long before she changed her tune and lamented that violence flowed so easily off our tongues and out of our pews, even for so great a cause as the abolition of slavery.

★ ★ ★

Music moves us. It can take us out of our seat, hands raised in worship. And it can take us all the way to the field of battle, often failing to prepare us for the solemn task ahead. The songs Christians sing in worship, and the music they listen to throughout the week, can and should have a profound influence in our lives. Sung,

12. Julia Ward Howe is profiled on page 120.

chanted, and even shouted, words all have power—either to create or destroy. Let song be recognized for its impact on our individual and collective formation as followers of Jesus, and may it always contribute to that reality.

"Sung, chanted, and even shouted, words all have power—either to create or destroy."

Appendix 8

Christian Statements on War

In order to cultivate a people who are capable of peace, it is important to make clear those convictions that restrain our tendency to violence. Many churches throughout the thousands of years of our history have made explicit their commitments in times that threaten to spiral toward war. By including the following doctrinal statements from various churches I am not necessarily agreeing with them. For a far more comprehensive resource documenting what Christian churches have said about war, see *Words of Conscience* (Washington, DC: National Interreligious Service Board for Conscientious Objectors, 1980), published by Shawn Perry with the Center on Conscience in War.[1]

"To be able to walk the narrow path of peace, we need to develop robust and realistic perspectives about war."

In the collection that follows, I have tried to allow the faith commitments themselves to dictate the order in which they were included—moving from more explicit and formulaic statements on war, to less concrete. I was surprised to find that the noncreedal Southern Baptists held to a more specific and detailed set of criteria on war than does the older Lutheran Church. Behind these sets of criteria are volumes and centuries of debate over the nature of the relationship between

1. It has been far too long since the center updated the tenth edition, which I personally relied upon during my conversion, detailed in my book *Reborn on the Fourth of July* (Downers Grove, IL: InterVarsity, 2012). Go to http://www.centeronconscience.org to support their efforts to publish an updated version for the twenty-first-century church in America.

just war and pacifism, on which I have a number of thoughts. But this is not a book about theological debates; it is a book about human lives and their ability to aid in those debates. The lists of criteria I include below can help to navigate those kinds of discussions. Besides, there are better books to guide that kind of discernment, the most invaluable of which is Daniel Bell's *Just War as Christian Discipleship* (Grand Rapids, MI: Brazos, 2009).

Finally, consider the just war criteria outlined below to be only samples of the many and varying beliefs in the wide array of Christian traditions on war. Given the evolutionary nature of modern war, most traditions will find it necessary to continually revise their commitments. In fact, many churches did just that after witnessing the destructive power of nuclear bombs.[2] Therefore, the commitments below should not be seen as final and comprehensive by any means. As war shifts its shapes and forms, so too must our understanding and approach to these commitments.[3] To be able to walk the narrow path of peace, we need to develop robust and realistic perspectives about war. First and foremost we must appreciate the actual lives of military people of faith, but we must also acknowledge that as followers of Jesus we cannot always live up to our good intentions.

Roman Catholics make up a significant proportion of the global church and have a highly developed sense of centralized authority. Headed by the pope in Rome, Catholics abide by a fairly detailed set of beliefs outlined in an official catechism, or summary of their theological beliefs. Laid out very logically by the model of the Ten Commandments, the official church teaching on war and violence is found under the section

2. "Nuclear pacifism" cropped up during the Cold War, in which the United States and Russia discovered their mutually assured destruction—if one detonated a bomb, the other would follow, leaving both nations sure to disappear no matter who struck first. In fact, the Roman Catholic Church became much more pacific in light of humankind's discovery that nations could literally destroy the world that God created.

3. On the subject of the evolution of war and peace, the authoritative texts are Roland H. Bainton, *Christian Attitudes toward War and Peace: A Historical Survey and Critical Re-Evaluation* (Eugene, OR: Wipf & Stock Publishers, 2008) and John H. Yoder, *Christian Attitudes to War, Peace, and Revolution* (Grand Rapids, MI: Brazos Press; 2009).

covering the fifth commandment, against killing. The following is paraphrased from Section III ("Safeguarding Peace"), found in paragraph number 2309. Catholics believe that a just war is one in which:

- The damage inflicted by the aggressor on the nation or community of nations must be lasting, grave, and certain.
- All other means of putting an end to it must have been shown to be impractical or ineffective.
- There must be serious prospects of success.
- The use of arms must not produce evils and disorders graver than the evil to be eliminated. The power of modern means of destruction weighs very heavily in evaluating this condition.

Southern Baptists are the largest Protestant denomination in North America and have the closest to what many scholars call the classical tenets of just war doctrine; they follow the developments by Christian theologians from as early as Augustine of Hippo and Thomas Aquinas. Some features, like noncombatant immunity and legitimate authority, are modern additions. As Southern Baptists are noncreedal and do not often abide by written convictions, this set of criteria, from the Southern Baptist Ethics and Religious Liberty Commission of the Southern Baptist Convention, is noteworthy:

- A just war must have a just cause. War is only permissible when it is done to resist aggression and to defend victims.
- A just war must have a just intent. Securing justice is the only acceptable motive.
- A just war must be a last resort. All other opportunities for resolution should have been rejected or have failed.
- A just war must have legitimate authority. In America's case, approval by Congress is necessary.
- A just war must have limited, or achievable, goals. Annihilation of an enemy or total destruction of a civilization is not acceptable as a goal.

- A just war must be proportional to its objectives. The good gained should justify the cost in lives and injuries.
- A just war must have noncombatant immunity. War should not be targeted at civilians and should seek to minimize inadvertent civilian casualties.[4]

Lutherans are also well represented in North America. Their roots trace back to the earliest Protestant reformer, Martin Luther, a German. Interestingly, Luther was named after Martin of Tours after being born on the saint's feast day. Lutheran distinctives arise out of their emphasis on the grace of God. In reference to war, the Augsburg Confession (Articles IV and XVI), to which Lutheran denominations adhere, asks the following questions to discern a just war:

- Is a war being fought under legitimate authority?
- Is it being conducted within the framework of international agreement?
- Is it being waged in the interest of vindicating some obvious right that has suffered outrage?
- Have all peaceful means of achieving a settlement been exhausted?
- Is the destruction incurred excessive in terms of the goals to be achieved?
- Is it being waged with good intentions, or has it been undertaken for purposes of aggression?
- Will the results achieved by engaging in hostilities provide greater opportunity for justice and freedom to prevail than if such a war had not been entered into?

Friends (Quakers) are often confused with Anabaptist groups from the Radical Reformation, but were actually an offshoot of the English Reformation, about a hundred years later. Known by their silent worship, in which they allow the Spirit to speak through congregants

---

4. From http://www.bpnews.net/bpnews.asp?id=11777, accessed June 2, 2013.

unimpeded by formal liturgy (or even Scripture reading, for some groups), Quakers have long been known for their pacifist convictions. The following Advice on Conscription and War[5] urges Friends:

- To support Young Friends and others who express their opposition to conscription either by nonregistration, or by registration as conscientious objectors. We warmly approve civil disobedience under Divine compulsion as an honorable testimony fully in keeping with the history and practices of Friends.
- To recognize that the military is not consistent with Christ's example of redemptive love, and that participation, even in a noncombatant capacity, weakens the testimony of our whole Society. Nevertheless, we hold in respect and sympathetic understanding all those men who in good conscience choose to enter the armed forces.
- To extend our religious concern and assistance to all conscientious objectors who may fall outside the narrow definition of the Selective Service Act of 1948.
- To avoid engaging in any trade, business, or profession directly contributing to the military system; and the purchase of government war bonds or stock certificates in war industries.
- To consider carefully the implication of paying those taxes, a major portion of which goes for military purposes.
- To ask our Quaker schools and colleges to refuse to accept military training units or contracts, or military subsidies for scientific research, and to advise Young Friends not to accept military training in other institutions.
- To create a home and family atmosphere in which the ways of love and reconciliation are so central that the resort to violence in any relationship is impossible.

---

5. Based on a meeting representing Friends in the United States, held at Earlham College, Richmond, Indiana, July 20-22, 1948. Also printed in *Quakers and the Draft*, by Charles Walker (Philadelphia, PA: Friends Coordinating Committee on Peace, 1968).

- To help develop the institutions, methods, and attitudes necessary to a harmonious and peaceful world; to replace political anarchy, national sovereignty and war by law.

Mennonites have their roots in the sixteenth-century Radical Reformation, which also eventually gave birth to Amish, Hutterite, and Brethren groups, many of which are today commonly referred to as historic peace churches. Neither Protestant nor Catholic, Mennonites were persecuted and fled from country to country for generations, many coming to settle in North and South America. Like the Baptists, Mennonites are not creedal, but they do summarize their convictions in confessions of faith. On the subject of war, Article 22 of the *Confession of Faith in a Mennonite Perspective* states:

> As followers of Jesus, we participate in his ministry of peace and justice. He has called us to find our blessing in making peace and seeking justice. We do so in a spirit of gentleness, willing to be persecuted for righteousness' sake. As disciples of Christ, we do not prepare for war, or participate in war or military service. The same Spirit that empowered Jesus also empowers us to love enemies, to forgive rather than to seek revenge, to practice right relationships, to rely on the community of faith to settle disputes, and to resist evil without violence.
>
> Led by the Spirit, and beginning in the church, we witness to all people that violence is not the will of God. We witness against all forms of violence, including war among nations, hostility among races and classes, abuse of children and women, violence between men and women, abortion, and capital punishment. [6]

United Methodists, another prominent denomination in the United States, trace their origins to a renewal in the Church of England in the

6. From http://www.mennolink.org/doc/cof/summary.html, accessed June 2, 2013.

eighteenth century, in which personal experience of faith was emphasized. Early leaders John and Charles Wesley found significant support in the American colonies. The United Methodist Church's 2004 *Book of Discipline* balances the interests of both pacifism and just war, respecting the sometimes conflicting convictions held among its members.

> We deplore war and urge the peaceful settlement of all disputes among nations. From the beginning, the Christian conscience has struggled with the harsh realities of violence and war, for these evils clearly frustrate God's loving purposes for humankind. We yearn for the day when there will be no more war and people will live together in peace and justice. Some of us believe that war, and other acts of violence, are never acceptable to Christians. We also acknowledge that many Christians believe that, when peaceful alternatives have failed, the force of arms may regretfully be preferable to unchecked aggression, tyranny and genocide. We honor the witness of pacifists who will not allow us to become complacent about war and violence. We also respect those who support the use of force, but only in extreme situations and only when the need is clear beyond reasonable doubt, and through appropriate international organizations. We urge the establishment of the rule of law in international affairs as a means of elimination of war, violence, and coercion in these affairs.

Appendix 9

Soldier Saints

Bold print indicates they are profiled in this book.

1. Nereus and Achileus (d. second century)—martyrs
2. Ammonius and Moseus (d. 250)—martyrs
3. Nestor (d. 250)—martyr
4. Mercurius (d. 250)—martyr
5. Christopher [Menas] (d. 251)—martyr
6. **Maurice and the Theban Legion** (d. 287)—martyrs
7. **Sebastian** (d. 288)—martyr
8. **Maximilian of Tebessa** (d. 295)—martyr
9. **Marcellus of Tangier** (d. 298)—martyr
10. Luxurius (d. 300)—martyr
11. Emeterius and Chelidonius (d. 300)—martyrs
12. Callistratus (d. 300)—martyr
13. Fidelis, Exantus, and Carpophorus (d. 300)—martyrs
14. Julius the Veteran (d. 302)—martyr
15. **George of Palestine** (d. 303)—martyr
16. Victor the Moor (d. 303)—martyr
17. Nabor and Felix (d. 303)—martyrs
18. **Sergius and Bacchus** (d. 303)—martyrs
19. Acacius (d. 303)—martyr
20. Procopius of Scythopolis (d. 303)—martyr
21. Typasius the Veteran (d. 304)—martyr

22. Gereon (d. 304)—martyr
23. Andrew the General (d. 305)—martyr
24. Theodore of Amasea (d. 306)—martyr
25. Demetrius of Thessaloniki (d. 306)—martyr
26. Varus (d. 307)—martyr
27. Theagenes (d. 308)—martyr
28. Menas the Soldier [Christopher] (d. 309)—martyr
29. Theodore the General (d. 319)—martyr
30. **Pachomius of Thebes** (d. 348)
31. Juventinus and Maximinus (d. 363)—martyrs
32. **Martin of Tours** (d. 397)
33. Victricius (d. 407)
34. Valeriano (d. fifth century)
35. **Francis of Assisi** (d. 1226)
36. **Joan of Arc** (d. 1431)—martyr
37. **John of God** (d. 1550)
38. **Ignatius of Loyola** (d. 1556)
39. **Camillus of Lellis** (d. 1614)
40. **John Vianney** (d. 1859)
41. **Franz Jägerstätter** (d. 1943)—martyr

Bibliography

In my research on this book, and in the list of books that follows here, I privilege soldiers' own accounts of war above those written by otherwise trustworthy and gifted writers who do not have experience in the military. First, I include a list of veteran biographies and books authored by veterans. The final group is of other books that I have consulted and sometimes cite in this book.

I do not necessarily share the same convictions as some of these authors and books. Some are more adamantly pacifist or concretely patriotic than I am. However, I value each of these works as conversation partners in the dialogue I am hoping to cultivate around Christians, soldiering, and citizenship. They may or may not agree with how I have interpreted the profiles in this book, though I pray the concern and hope for healthy discourse is genuinely mutual. You can also check *http://loganmehllaituri.com/recommendations* for my reflections on books, movies, music, and other resources for understanding and recovering the intersection between Christian faith and military service.

Stories referenced in this book:

Autobiographies

Berrigan, Philip. *Fighting the Lamb's War: Skirmishes with the American Empire, the Autobiography of Philip Berrigan*. Munroe, ME: Common Courage Press, 1996.

Casteel, Joshua. *Letters from Abu Ghraib*. Ithaca, NY: Essay Press, 2008.

Mahedy, William P. *Out Of The Night: The Spiritual Journey of Vietnam Vets*. Knoxville, TN: Radix Books, 2004.

Mejía, Camilo. *Road from ar Ramadi: The Private Rebellion of Staff Sergeant Mejía: An Iraq War Memoir.* Chicago, IL: Haymarket Books, 2008.

Olin, John C. and Joseph F. O'Callaghan, trans. *The Autobiography of St. Ignatius of Loyola, with Related Documents*. New York: Fordham University Press, 1992.

Perkins, John. *Let Justice Roll Down*. Ventura, CA: Regal, 1976.

Sampson, Francis L. *Look Out Below! A Story of the Airborne by a Paratrooper Padre*. Sweetwater, TN: 101st Airborne Division Association, 1989.

York, Alvin C. and Tom J. Skeyhill. *Sergeant York: His Own Life Story and War Diary*. Garden City, NY: Doubleday, Doran and Company, Inc., 1928.

Biographies

Benedict, Terry L. *The Conscientious Objector*. Cinequest, 2010, DVD. [Desmond Doss]

Bonaventure, St. *The Life of Saint Francis of Assisi*. New York, NY: Paulist Press, 1978.

Lee, Dallas. *The Cotton Patch Evidence: The Story of Clarence Jordan and the Koinonia Farm Experiment.* Eugene, OR: Wipf & Stock, 2011.

Peek, Susan. *A Soldier Surrenders: The Conversion of Saint Camillus de Lellis*. San Francisco, CA: Ignatius Press, 2007.

Pernoud, Regine. *Joan of Arc: By Herself and Her Witnesses*. New York, NY: Dorset, 1988.

——. *Martin of Tours: Soldier, Bishop, Saint*. San Francisco, CA: Ignatius Press, 2006.

Weimberg, Gary and Catherine Ryan. *Soldiers of Conscience*. New York, NY: Docuramafilms, 2009, DVD.

Zahn, Gordon C. *In Solitary Witness*. Springfield, IL: Templegate Pub, 1986. [Franz Jägerstätter]

Stories not included in this book:

Autobiographies

Arnett, Edward M. *A Different Kind of War Story: A Conscientious Objector in World War II*. Xlibris Corporation, 2012.

Benimoff, R. with E. Conant. *Faith Under Fire: An Army Chaplain's Memoir*. New York, NY: Crown, 2009.

Cash, C. H. *A Table in the Presence*. New York, NY: Ballantine, 2005.

Iraq Veterans Against the War. *After Action Review: A Collection of Writing and Artwork by Veterans of the Global War on Terror*. Warrior Writers, 2011.

———. *Move, Shoot, Communicate: A Collection of Creative Writing*. Burlington, VT: Warrior Writers, 2007.

———. *Re-Making Sense: A Collection of Artwork*. Burlington, VT: Warrior Writers, 2008.

Iraq Veterans Against the War, with Aaron Glantz. *Winter Soldier: Iraq and Afghanistan: Eyewitness Accounts of the Occupations*. Chicago, IL: Haymarket Books, 2008.

Kovic, Ron. *Born on the Fourth of July*. New York: Akashic Books, 2005.

Mehl-Laituri, Logan. *Reborn on the Fourth of July: The Challenge of Faith, Patriotism, and Conscience*. Downer's Grove, IL: InterVarsity, 2012.

O'Callahan, Joseph T. *I Was Chaplain on the Franklin*. New York, NY: Macmillan, 1956.

Snively, S. *Heaven in the Midst of Hell: A Quaker Chaplain's View of the War in Iraq*. Jamul, CA: Raven Oaks, 2010.

Hagiographies and almanacs

Cook, Jane H. *Stories of Faith and Courage from the Revolutionary War*. Battlefields and Blessings series. Chattanooga, TN: God & Country Press, 2007.

Cook, Jane Hampton, John Croushorn, and Jocelyn Green. *Stories of Faith and Courage from the War in Iraq and Afghanistan*. Battlefields and Blessings series. Chattanooga, TN: God & Country Press, 2009.

Bennett, William J. and J. T. Cribb. *The American Patriot's Almanac: Daily Readings on America*. Nashville, TN: Thomas Nelson, 2008.

DC Talk. *Martyrs Who Stood for Jesus, the Ultimate Jesus Freaks*. Minneapolis, MN: Bethany, 2005.

———. *Revolutionaries Who Changed Their World, Fearing God not Man*. Minneapolis, MN: Bethany, 2005.

Dear, John and William H. McNichols. *You Will Be My Witnesses: Saints, Prophets, And Martyrs*. Maryknoll, NY: Orbis Books, 2006.

Delaney, J.J. *Dictionary of Saints*. New York, NY: Doubleday, 2005.

Foxe, John, and W. Berry. *Foxe's Book of Martyrs*. Old Tappan, NJ: Revell, 1999.

Mac, Toby and Michael Tait. *Under God*. Minneapolis, MN: Bethany, 2004.

Spivey, Larkin. *Stories of Faith and Courage from the Vietnam War*. Battlefields and Blessings series. Chattanooga, TN: God & Country Press, 2011.

———. *Stories of Faith and Courage from World War II*. Battlefields and Blessings series. Chattanooga, TN: God & Country Press, 2009.

St. James, Rebecca and Mary E. DeMuth. *Sister Freaks: Stories of Women Who Gave Up Everything for God*. New York, NY: FaithWords, 2005.

Tuley, Terry. *Stories of Faith and Courage from the Civil War*. Battlefields and Blessings series. Chattanooga, TN: God & Country Press, 2006.

Van Braght, J. *Martyrs Mirror: The Story of Seventeen Centuries of Christian Martyrdom from the Time of Christ to A.D. 1660*. Scottdale, PA: Herald Press, 1938.

Woodward, K. L. *Making Saints: How the Catholic Church Determines Who Becomes a Saint, Who Doesn't, and Why*. New York, NY: Simon and Schuster, 1990.

Veterans on war

Cantey, Daniel. "Can the Christian Serve in the Military? A Veteran Reflects on the Commensurability of the Christian Life and the Military Ethic," *Journal of the Society for Christian Ethics*, Volume 32, Number 2.

Cortright, David. *Soldiers in Revolt: GI Resistance During the Vietnam War*. Chicago, IL: Haymarket Books, 2005.

Finn, James. *A Conflict of Loyalties*. New York, NY: Pegasus, 1968.

Grossman, David. *On Killing: The Psychological Cost of Learning to Kill in War and Society*. New York, NY: Back Bay Books, 1996.

Jordan, Clarence. *Cotton Patch Gospel: The Complete Collection*. Macon, GA: Smyth & Helwys Publishing, 2012.

Marshall, SLA. *Men Against Fire: The Problem of Battle Command*. Norman, OK: University of Oklahoma Press, 2000.

Mauldin, Bill. *Up Front*. New York, NY: Norton, 1995.

Moore, Hal G. and J. L. Galloway. *We Are Soldiers Still: A Journey Back to the Battlefields of Vietnam*. New York, NY: Harper Perennial, 2009.

Scott, Wilbur. *Vietnam Veterans Since the War: The Politics of PTSD, Agent Orange, and the National Memorial*. Norman, OK: University of Oklahoma, 2004.

Zinn, Howard. *Just War*. Milan, Italy: Charta, 2006.

Other books cited or consulted

Bainton, Roland H. *Christian Attitudes Toward War and Peace: A Historical Survey and Critical Re-Evaluation*. Eugene, OR: Wipf & Stock Publishers, 2008.

Catechism of the Catholic Church. Vatican City: United States Catholic Conference, 2000.

Claiborne, Shane. *The Irresistible Revolution: Living as An Ordinary Radical.* Grand Rapids, MI: Zondervan, 2006.

Collins, Ace. *Stories Behind the Hymns That Inspire America.* Grand Rapids, MI: Zondervan, 2003.

Coogan, Michael D. *A Brief Introduction to the Old Testament: The Hebrew Bible in its Context.* London, UK: Oxford, 2009.

Ebel, Jonathan H. *Faith in the Fight: Religion and the American Soldier in the Great War.* Princeton, NJ: Princeton University Press, 2010.

Freemantle, Anne, ed. *A Treasury of Early Christianity.* New York: Viking Press, 1953.

Hauerwas, Stanley and Jean Vanier. *Living Gently in a Violent World: The Prophetic Witness of Weakness.* Downers Grove, IL: InterVarsity, 2008.

Hopkins, Mary R. *Men of Peace: World War II Conscientious Objectors.* Caye Caulker, Belize: Producciciones de la Hamaca, 2009.

Kern, Kathleen. *In Harm's Way: A History of Christian Peacemaker Teams.* Eugene, OR: Cascade, 2009.

MacDonald, Patricia. *God and Violence; Biblical Resources for Living in a Small World.* Scottdale, PA: Herald Press, 2004.

McClendon, James. *Biography as Theology: How Life Stories Can Remake Today's Theology.* Eugene, OR: Wipf & Stock, 2002.

Nakashima-Brock, Rita, and Gabriella Lettini. *Soul Repair: Recovering from Moral Injury after War.* Boston, MA: Beacon, 2012.

Perry, Shawn. *Words of Conscience; Religious Statements on Conscientious Objection.* Washington, D.C.: National Interreligious Service Board for Conscientious Objectors (NISBCO), 1980.

Romero, Oscar. *The Violence of Love.* Rifton, NY: Plough, 2011.

Schmitt, Eric. "Soft Economy Aids Recruiting Effort," *New York Times,* 22 Sept. 2003.

Thompson, D. A., and D. Wetterstrom. *Beyond the Yellow Ribbon: Ministering to Returning Combat Veterans.* Nashville, TN: Abingdon Press, 2009.

Tick, Edward. *War and the Soul: Healing Our Nation's Veterans from Post-Traumatic Stress Disorder*. Wheaton, IL: Quest Books, 2005.

Tollefson, James W. *The Strength Not to Fight: Conscientious Objectors of the Vietnam War—in Their Own Words*. Boston: Little, Brown, 1993.

Unknown. "Saint Marcellus: Military Martyr." *In Communion*. Orthodox Peace Fellowship, 27 Oct. 2007.

Verkamp, Bernard J. *Moral Treatment of Returning Warriors in Early Medieval and Modern Times*. Scranton, PA: University of Scranton Press, 2006.

Walker, Charles. *Quakers and the Draft*. Philadelphia, PA: Friends Coordinating Committee on Peace, 1968.

Wilhelm, Paul. *Civilian Public Servants: A Report on 210 World War II Conscientious Objectors*. Washington, DC: National Interreligious Service Board for Conscientious Objectors, 1990.

Yoder, John H. *Christian Attitudes to War, Peace, and Revolution*. Grand Rapids, MI: Brazos Press, 2009.

Military regulations governing chaplaincy

http://www.militaryonesource.mil/non-medical-counseling/service-providers?content_id=268837.

- Army Regulation (AR) 165-1, "Army Chaplain Corps Activities"
- Army Field Manual (FM) 1-05, "Religious Support"
- Air Force Policy Directive (AFPD) 52-1, "Chaplain Service"
- Secretary of the Navy Instruction (SECNAVINST) 1730.7D, "Religious Ministry within the Department of the Navy"
- Marine Corps Order (MCO) 1730.6D, "Command Religious Programs in the Marine Corps"
- Fleet Marine Force Manual (FMFM) 3-61, "Ministry in Combat"
- Commandant Instruction (COMDTINST) M1730.4B, "Religious Ministries within the Coast Guard," 30 Aug. 1994

Acknowledgments

This book would not have been possible without innumerable contributions of family, friends, and enemies alike. Besides my editor, Byron Rempel-Burkholder, there have been many helpers along the way. Shane Claiborne and Jonathan Wilson-Hartgrove have continued to support my writing and other vocational calls around military service and Christian faith.

This book is the fruit of at least six years of reading, listening, reflecting, and worshiping with a peculiarly martial community of faith that is Centurions Guild. Those who have helped nurture that community were invaluable not only to producing the book but to sustaining me personally. Special thanks go to Alex Arzuaga, Sara Beining, Andy Bell, Kyle and Jessica Caldwell, Zach and Laurel Cornelius, Will Fisher, Joe Gibson, Jason and Rhonda Vance, and Nate and Angela Wildermuth. I am also grateful to the soldiers whose letters are featured in the graphics throughout the book, as well as civilian allies Titus Peachey, Mike Griffin, and Shawn Storer.

Several good friends endured the unrefined and awkward wording of the soldier saint profiles. Over food, festivities, and conversation in the eighth week of Ordinary Time after Pentecost 2012, they helped me make good decisions about the structure and content of the book. I owe much gratitude to Sarah Campbell, Niel Hoefs, Lucas Martin, Jeremy Stainthorp-Berggren, and Naaman Wood.

The following autumn, leading into Advent, a few seminarians attended a series of Bible studies that laid the groundwork for the Warriors of the Bible section. Their exegetical and interpretive expertise significantly improved my own ability to read the Old Testament

without wanting to rip several chapters out due to pacifist frustration. Promising exegetes, pastors, and theologians Lauren Greenspan, Amber Noel, Tyler Smoot, and Cindy Spicer were instrumental in guarding the faith against my heterodox inclinations.

Then, just a few days after Epiphany 2013, more friends attended a reading at Mercury Studio in Durham, North Carolina, to hear some of the completed profiles, including many of the patriot pacifists in the third segment. Their pleasant surprise at some of the connections I discovered and tried to weave together inspired and challenged me. Thanks go to Jessica Andrews, Sara Blaine, Banks Clark, Katie DeConto, Brandon Hudson, Alaina Kleinbeck, Laura Lysen, and Tiffany Prest, for sharing their reflections with me.

Newer friends have helped elaborate, correct, and nuance some of the profiles. Beth Pyles helped with the Tom Fox profile, and Mike Angell with Rev. Bill Mahedy's. For Camilo's, Nate's, and Zach's profiles, I worked from personal conversations and received valued feedback from them. Zach found a number of excellent folks to profile and encouraged me throughout the project. That he is not listed as a coauthor is probably some kind of fraud, though the kind to which he refuses to object.

Finally, a few brave souls dared to read and return the manuscript to me with their suggested revisions and deletions. That they risked my wrath by placing a higher priority on quality over quantity (among other things) displayed their boundless character and virtue. Thanks especially to Russell Johnson, Ebony Grissom, Brian Gumm, Anna Masi, Andy Scott, and, most especially, to my tango partner, Laura E. Tardie.

Many of these dear friends made multiple contributions along the way. That so many lovely people committed so much time and energy is a testament not to my character, but to their own.

The Author

Logan Mehl-Laituri is a combat veteran who speaks and writes broadly about veterans' issues and Christian perspectives on militarism and nationalism. He served in the Iraq War as a forward observer for the artillery before applying to change his status to noncombatant conscientious objector. After his discharge in 2006 he worked in Palestine with Christian Peacemaker Teams and cofounded Centurions Guild, a community of Christian soldiers, veterans, and their allies. After earning a BA in human services from Hawaii Pacific University, he went on to receive a certificate in gender, theology, and ministry and a master of theological studies degree at Duke University. At Duke he served in a number of student veterans groups, convened the 2011 After the Yellow Ribbon conference on the effects of war on soldiers and veterans, and worked for a year as a cocoordinator of the Divinity School Women's Center. Logan has collaborated on *The Gospel of Rutba* (Orbis, 2012), as well as *Jesus, Bombs, and Ice Cream* (Zondervan, 2012) and authored *Reborn on the Fourth of July* (InterVarsity, 2012). He is a communicant of St. Joseph's Episcopal Church in Durham, North Carolina, where he lives. His website is loganmehllaituri.com.

Notes

Notes

Notes

Notes

Notes

Notes